BOSTON'S BALLPARKS AND ARENAS

Northeastern University Press   BOSTON

Published by University Press of New England   HANOVER & LONDON

ALAN E. FOULDS

Boston's
Ballparks & Arenas

Northeastern University Press
Published by
University Press of New England
One Court Street, Lebanon, NH 03766
www.upne.com
© 2005 by Alan E. Foulds
Printed in the United States of American
5 4 3 2 1

Library of Congress Cataloging-in-Publication Data
Foulds, Alan E.
Boston's ballparks and arenas / Alan E. Foulds.
    p.   cm.
Includes bibliographical references and index.
ISBN 1–58465–409–0 (cloth : alk. paper)
1. Stadiums—Massachusetts—Boston. 2. Arenas—
Massachusetts—Boston. I. Title.
GV415.F68 2005
796'.06'80974461—dc22   2004019240

To my family,
which is always there
to offer whatever help
is needed, and to my
uncle, Sam Foulds,
whose love of sports
history rubbed off
on me.

CONTENTS

ILLUSTRATIONS

INTRODUCTION

A SPORTS HUB

Boston has been called the "hub of the universe" and the "Athens of America," chiefly due to its renowned universities, hospitals, museums, and symphony orchestra. It truly is a hub of cultural and business activities for Massachusetts, and, to a certain extent, all of New England. Within the confines of the Commonwealth of Massachusetts, as well as southern New Hampshire and northern Rhode Island, there is also a special reverence for its sports teams. The city is the epicenter of eastern Massachusetts—stretching to Andover on the north, west to Worcester, and south to Fall River—and has been well represented in nearly every sports venture that has ever been launched. In baseball, for instance, Boston is the only city that has had a major league team continuously since 1871, when the National Association began. The Bruins were the first American team to join the ranks of major league hockey in the days when "National" in National Hockey League meant Canada. The Celtics are one of only two charter members of the NBA still playing in their original cities.

The Hub has had four National Football League franchises as well as representatives in four different American Football Leagues. Greater Boston has had soccer teams in seven leagues, stretching back to 1894. Dotting the sports landscape also are lacrosse, team tennis, and even teamball teams.

With each entry has come a venue in which to play. Some became sports shrines, such as Fenway Park and Boston Garden. Others, like Braves Field, live on in memory and in a reduced form. Some have disappeared altogether. Today one would be hard pressed to find the Congress Street Grounds, a stadium built to last—but which only lasted two seasons.

The Huntington Avenue Grounds, the only field other than Fenway that the Red Sox have ever called home, hosted the first modern World Series (where the locals defeated the Pittsburgh Pirates). The field is but a memory, but it is marked with a plaque on the wall of Northeastern University's Cabot Physical Education Center.

Just forty miles west, the Worcester County Agricultural Fair Grounds on Sever Street was once the home of a National League franchise, but is hard to find now, even for Worcesterites.

Fifty miles south of the city and twenty miles north, soccer-specific stadiums were built to house professional teams in the 1920s. That era was long before politicians talked of "soccer moms."

Within the city limits of Boston there have been six major league baseball parks, as well as a minor league field. Professional football and soccer have been played in another two stadiums, and hockey—in the form of two major and three minor league teams—has been staged in three arenas. Suburban Foxborough is home to the New England Patriots; the twenty-first-century stadium replaced its thirty-year-old predecessor. Within a fifty-mile radius of Boston there have been professional sports at several other venues as well.

FROM TOGAS TO TROLLEYS TO TAILGATERS

The word "stadium" comes from the Greek *stadion*, a distance measure of about six hundred feet, an early standard for foot races. Thus, a place where the races were held was known as a "stadium." Gradually, those early stadiums made accommodations for spectators, in the form of tiered seating. Most prominent among the early venues was the Olympic Stadium, located in Olympia, Greece, and home to the ancient Olympic Games. They were staged there as early as 776 B.C. Similarly, the stadium at Delphi hosted the quadrennial Pythian Games.

Stadiums grew to be a part of a community's life. The Coliseum in Rome, built in A.D. 80, is a good example of their evolution, living on long after the fall of the Roman Empire. In the United States, stadiums appeared in the middle of the nineteenth century with the advent of professional sports.

In the years immediately following the Civil War, sport was considered the province of the gentleman. The workingman had no time for such frivolity. In the 1870s and 1880s dynamics changed. The Industrial Revolution caused a shift of the population from farm to factory and from the country to the city. Team sports were the outlet of the masses. Those born in the United States often favored baseball, while many immigrants preferred soccer. Soccer, in turn, spawned American football. Large industrial firms located in major cities encouraged the creation of sports teams to help worker morale. In many cases the firms provided playing fields.

In the late 1860s a new phenomenon was born. Amateur baseball teams ventured from their own backyards to play like-minded clubs from other cities. In 1869 the Cincinnati Red Stockings became the first truly professional team. Players were paid an average of a thousand dollars per season. The team was not a business success. In its first year it reported revenues of about twenty-nine thousand dollars, and expenses of about twenty-nine thousand dollars. In fact, the net profit was under five dollars. It was, however, a success on the field, beating nearly every challenger. More importantly, it became a source of pride for the city. Spectators filled the stands in support of the hometown team. Other cities wanted the same, and new professional teams sprang up around the countryside.

That era saw cheaply built stadiums. Teams were not good financial bets, and they were transitory. That changed in the 1880s. With the advent of the National League came stability; with stability came profitability, and improvement in the parks reflected the movement. Style was added. Often, upper decks and press boxes were incorporated into the designs. In those days sports venues were generally built within city limits, where the highest concentration of potential customers lived. According to the 1900 U.S. census, 20 percent of all Massachusetts residents lived within Boston. Fans traveled to the games by public transportation, or on foot.

About 1910, sports parks entered a new era. Small stadiums, such as the South End Grounds in Boston, with only forty-five hundred seats, were dying. Replacing them were sports palaces like Braves Field, large enough to seat forty thousand. In the first decade of the twentieth century major league attendance rose an astounding 88 percent, and the new seating capacity was designed to accommodate the growth. Sports had become big business.

The next great change came in the 1950s. After the Second World War—with prosperity high, returning veterans to house, and a baby boom to accommodate—an exodus to the suburbs began. As the state's population rose, Boston's fell. According to the 1960 census, only 13 percent of Massachusetts residents called Boston home. This city-to-suburb trend was reflected nationwide.

As the population moved, so too did sports teams. Baseball and football fields, as well as basketball and hockey arenas, were no longer confined to the inner cities. Throughout the United States, megaplexes were constructed, sometimes miles from downtown. Stadiums often were no longer nestled against city buildings, situated on trolley lines. The new sports palaces were springing up on highways, surrounded by acres of asphalt. Bars and restaurants that had grown alongside the parks, catering to those coming from or going to the games, were on the wane. Instead their patrons became "tailgaters," often meeting in stadium parking lots hours before game time to eat, drink, and socialize with other fans. Ticket holders were no longer traveling by trolley, subway, or foot. The auto was king.

In Boston, that movement was slower than in other parts of the country. Fenway Park lives on today as an inner-city park, much as it was when it opened in 1912. Even Boston Garden, built in 1928, was replaced by its successor facility almost exactly on the same ground, in downtown Boston. Commuter trains run to the back door of the new arena, and the subway stop is across the street. Basketball and hockey fans still arrive by rapid transit.

As professional football became an accepted major league sport, however, the Boston area followed the national trend, then led it. Foxboro Stadium was built several miles south of Boston, to house the Patriots. Much like stadiums around the country, it sat in a large parking lot. Although a train stopped nearby, its patrons, for the most part, drove there. In 2001 its successor, Gillette Stadium, took the trend one step further, to fully accommodate the automobile. Where Foxboro Stadium was built on available land and adapted to the environment, the building of Gillette Stadium required highway and access changes, reflecting full acceptance of the car. Several million dollars in road renovation were spent in conjunction with the construction of the park.

Over the course of a century and a half, as each of Greater Boston's teams found a home to hang its hat, or cleats, skates, or rackets, the landscape became dotted with active and retired professional sports venues. Some are widely known and some are not even recognized by those who work and shop at their sites today. Many have gained immortality in books and motion pictures, while some faded before the glory days ever arrived. In all cases these parks, stadiums, and arenas have a special hold on us, whether caused by the history or the shouts of the fans, the lights or the green, green grass. These places have housed the teams that New Englanders have cared about, as they carried Boston's banner across the continent and welcomed the world back to its doorstep.

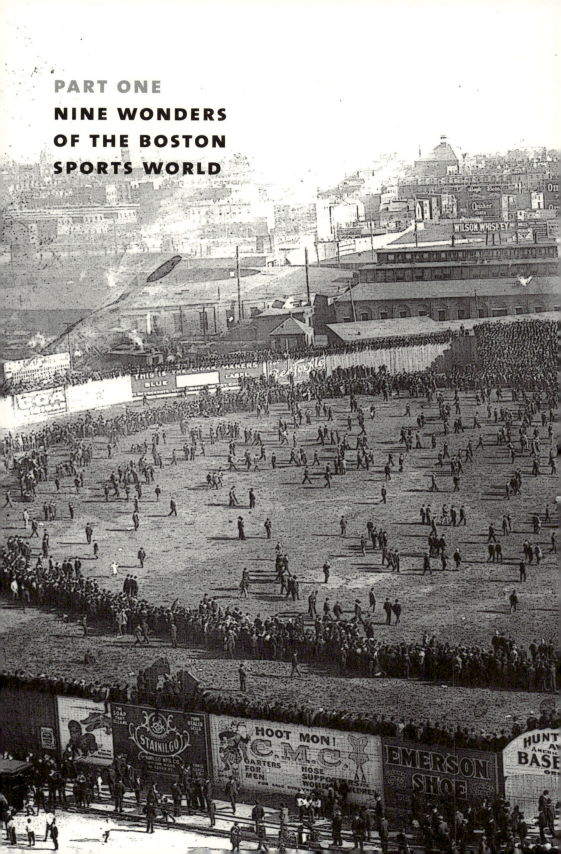

PART ONE

NINE WONDERS OF THE BOSTON SPORTS WORLD

FIGURE 1: Crowd in the grandstand of the South End Grounds; ca. 1890.
National Baseball Hall of Fame Library, Cooperstown, N.Y.

The City of Boston and its environs have hosted more than forty professional sports teams and events. Including high-school and college stadiums as well as town fields, these teams played in almost as many venues. Nine sites, however, stand out. These "major league nine" were not considered temporary homes, but were closely associated with the fortunes of both players and owners. No one can think of Boston Garden without picturing Bobby Orr sailing through the air and into immortality as his winning goal brought the Stanley Cup back to the hockey-mad city for the first time in twenty-nine years. The Garden also conjures up ghosts of Johnny Most screaming, "Havlicek stole the ball!" Etched indelibly onto our collective sports memories at friendly Fenway is an image of Carlton Fisk waving a home-run ball fair as it sailed deep into the October night sky in the greatest ball game ever played. An earlier generation saw the incredible Ted Williams hit one last home

3

WHAT'S IN A NAME?

Stadium names in the nineteenth century were not as "official" as they are now. With today's stadiums and arenas sporting multimillion-dollar corporate logos it is hard to imagine the cavalier attitude baseball entities once had with regard to monikers. The South End Grounds, for instance, bore no sign proclaiming that name. It was as likely to be called the Walpole Street Grounds, Franklin Place, or even the Columbus Avenue Grounds. The Congress Street Grounds were sometimes referenced as Brotherhood Park. Dartmouth Street was often called Union Grounds—not to be confused with the park in the South End, which occasionally used that name.

run, but refuse to tip his hat, before hanging up his cleats. Even utilitarian Foxboro Stadium, formerly Sullivan Stadium and Schaefer Stadium before that, offered "snow angels" in a surreal grand finale at that concrete bowl on Route 1.

Nine sports arenas have played an integral part in history in a city rich with history on many fronts. From the nineteenth to the twenty-first centuries, the sports venues of Boston have developed an enduring heritage. From 1871, with the first game at a tiny, dusty ballpark tucked into the shadows of a railroad yard in the South End, to the long-awaited grand opening in 1995 of a new hockey and basketball arena at Causeway Street, these places have been as familiar to thousands of Bostonians as Faneuil Hall, Old Ironsides, Harvard, MIT, and maybe, in some cases, their own homes. In 2002 a dazzling twenty-first-century Gillette Stadium—to house the Super Bowl champion Patriots and soccer's Revolution—joined its older brethren. Its symbolic lighthouse replica, a nod to the New England locale, will undoubtedly witness scores of memorable moments.

Unlike some temporary homes, these nine have had staying power—usually lasting for at least a generation of fans, and sometimes hosting even the great-grandchildren of the original patrons. Due in large part to Yankee frugality, stadiums and arenas last a long time in New England. Boston's professional baseball teams have remained at their respective fields for an average of forty-three years, with Fenway housing its teams for over ninety (and still counting); the league average is only twenty-three years. The Boston Bruins played at their venerable Garden for sixty-eight years. When they left, they had been there more than twice

4

as long as twenty-four of hockey's other pro teams had been in existence.

The ballparks and arenas, monuments to the old town teams, have worn out and will continue to do so, but the events that took place on the base paths, the gridiron, or the ice live on in family stories, discussions around the water coolers, and in barrooms. Some of the memories are among the fans' happiest, some are poignant, some sad, and some are downright frustrating.

This is the story of Boston's most precious sports shrines.

5

1 SOUTH END GROUNDS

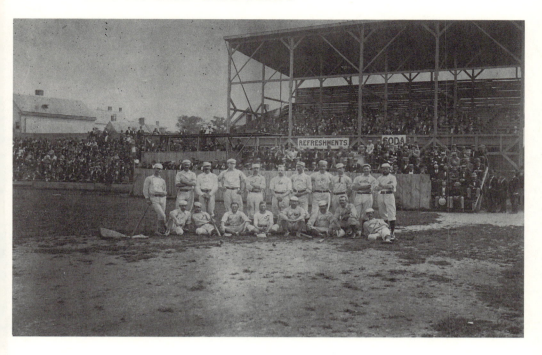

OPENED: April 7, 1871

CLOSED: February 9, 1929

FIELD MEASUREMENTS:

Left field 250 feet, Deep center field 450 feet, Right field 225 feet

Capacity: 2,500 to 5,800

TENANTS:

Boston Braves (National Association/National League);
baseball, 1871 to 1914

Boston Blues (Eastern Baseball League); *baseball, 1886*

Boston Beaneaters (American League of Professional Football
Clubs); *soccer, 1894*

Boston Wonder Workers (American Soccer League); *soccer, 1925 to 1929*

Boston Hubs (National Soccer League); *soccer, 1926*

For the first sixty years of professional outdoor sports the sure way to achieve "major league" status in the eyes of the public was to play at Boston's South End Grounds. Principally the home of the Boston Red Stockings, later known as the Boston Braves, it also at various times housed three soccer teams, a minor league baseball club, and Northeastern University athletics. The field was small by today's standards, and had nearly nothing in the way of amenities. Although a concession stand was in evidence from the beginning, rest rooms were not. The structure was hidden away on the fringes of the South End. Nestled up against the Boston and Providence Railroad tracks, the land was cheap. With cinders and smoke from the passing trains ever present, the site was not highly regarded as prime real estate. Yet because of those tracks and nearby streetcars the field was easily accessible for most Bostonians.

The train tracks comprised the western border, while a road then known as "Berlin Street" delineated the east. This latter thoroughfare would shortly be incorporated as part of Columbus Avenue. On the south was Walpole Street, while just outside the north wall was a railroad roundhouse. Beyond that structure was Camden Street.

The structure was of simple design and resembled many of the parks of the era. The main grandstand was quite boxy, containing approximately twenty-five rows of seats under the cover of the overhanging roof. The roof was held up by six supports. Angling out from the grandstand, paralleling the base paths from home plate, were sets of "bleaching seats," which were exposed to the elements. Tickets in the main grandstand cost fifty cents, while those in the bleachers only put the patron out a quarter.

"Bleaching seats," "bleaching boards," and "bleachers" were all terms used to describe seating out from under the roof of the grandstand. It was facetiously said that this exposed their occupants to potential bleaching by the sun. The term "bleachers" is still used today.

There was also plenty of room for standing. In fact, things were much less formal in the early days. If the designated areas for spectators filled up, people would simply spill into the outfield. Surrounding the park in a square was a wooden fence twelve feet high. Beneath the back of the grandstand on the Walpole Street side were two ticket booths; in those

(overleaf) FIGURE 2: Boston Red Stockings (Braves) and Philadelphia Athletics inside the South End Grounds; ca. 1872. *Courtesy of Boston Public Library, Print Department*

BASEBALL'S WRIGHT BROTHERS

George and Harry Wright were the first stars of Boston baseball. The sons of Sam Wright, a famous English cricketeer, they headed west with the idea of playing their father's game. Eventually making their way to Cincinnati, they switched sports and both joined up with the 1866 Cincinnati Red Stockings. That team built a reputation of invincibility over the next few years, under the captaincy of Harry. In 1870, however, team fortunes spiraled downward and the club's directors disbanded the team. The brothers came east to Boston and remained connected with New England baseball for over a decade.

In Boston Harry was given the title "captain," which meant he played on the team and managed it as well. He had a solid career as a player, but had a remarkable record as manager. His team won the pennant six years out of his eight at the helm. Its overall record in league play for that period was 347 wins and 108 losses.

Brother George stayed with the team during the same period, playing shortstop for most of the time. His hitting was better than most, with his batting average reaching as high as .387 one year.

After his retirement as a player George cofounded the Boston sporting goods supply firm Wright & Ditson, and also invested in both the Union Association and Players League teams in Boston.

days it was not uncommon for the team's owners to take a turn selling from the box office. Situated conveniently across Walpole Street was the home of the groundskeeper.

In the days following the Civil War and prior to 1871, many pro teams toured the country, but no formal league had been established. Although Boston was one of the hotbeds of the game and one of its birthplaces, the professional game had not arrived until the National Association of Professional Baseball Players formed.

The owners of a newly forming local team—which would operate as a franchise of the National Association—started on a grand scale. They leased land from the railroad, built their own park, and immediately set out to build a contender, as well. The famed Cincinnati Red Stockings had opted not to join the new association, and instead went dormant. Led by brothers George and Harry Wright, many of the team's stars came east and joined the new Boston franchise. Although they would later gain fame as the "Boston Braves," the new team even adopted the Cincinnati club's name, the "Red Stockings," as well as its uniform.

OPENING DAY, APRIL 7, 1871

Opening day, and the beginning of this city's love affair with the National Pastime, came on a beautiful, clear, and warm April 7, 1871, with fanfare. Well before the game, the streets outside the park were crowded, and the park filled to capacity before the opening pitch. To start things off an exhibition game was played between the Lowells and the Harvards. Then the anticipating crowd got what it had come to see. First the Picked Nine, a team of local high-level amateurs, took to the field to the sound of warm applause. Next came the "hometown" Red Stockings team, which was to carry Boston's baseball banner in games across the country throughout the summer; this time the crowd gave the entering team a rousing welcome. They looked quite impressive with their new team colors blazing, and the reporter for the *Boston Post* called their apparel, "The neatest uniform yet originated." It consisted of a white flannel shirt, knee breeches, a round cap with visor, and brilliant red stockings reaching all the way to the player's knees. Completing the outfit was a red belt, red necktie, and white canvas shoes. The name of the club was in a black semicircle over the breast pocket.

In a short ceremony Captain Harry Wright and the captain of the Picked Nine headed to the mound, where the umpire flipped a coin. The Picked Nine won the toss and chose to take the field first. Although the new Boston crew had been assembled only three weeks earlier, and were playing only a hastily gathered amateur contingent, the team made an impressive first showing. It won the game 41 to 10 but by all reports their fielding skills were beyond anything that had been seen in Boston before. The game boded well for league action.

A BAD START IN THE FIRST LEAGUE GAME

The first league game at home was played over a month later, after the team first made a western swing through upstate New York. On that trip, Boston had met and beaten the Troy club 9 to 5, but the Haymakers came back for revenge. The night before the May 16 match the Troy team arrived with scores of loyal supporters in tow, and put up at the United States Hotel. Electricity was in the Boston air as the "real" games were about to begin. Again the grandstand and bleachers overflowed as twenty-five hundred rabid fans filled every last inch of space in the grounds. As with the exhibition in April, the fans were excited but polite. When each "nine" entered the park it was greeted with warm applause. As was the practice in the National Association, the teams first had to agree on an umpire. The man chosen for the job was Mr. M. M. Rogers,

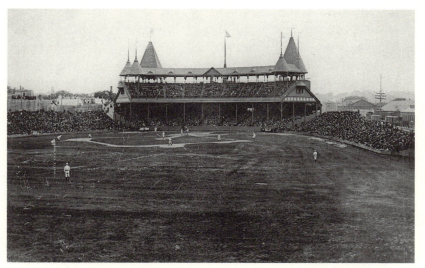

FIGURE 3: Grandstand of the South End Grounds, from center field; 1893.
Courtesy of the Bostonian Society/Old State House

a minor leaguer from the Star club of Brooklyn. The two team captains arrived at center field for the toss, and the game began. Boston's Harry Wright won the coin toss, but things went downhill from there. At day's end the Troy Haymakers were victorious by a score of 29–14.

Although the Red Stockings finished the first season in a disappointing third place out of nine, they actually compiled an impressive twenty and ten record. That placed them only one win behind the pennant-winning Athletics. The next year, though, they achieved a domination of the sport that actually contributed to the demise of this first professional league. In 1872 Boston finished on top, four games clear of its closest opponent, and eleven games ahead of the previous champions. The following year saw an even greater disparity as the Red Stockings, with a 52–18 record, finished seven and a half games ahead of the second-place team. In 1875, the last year the league played, Boston finished fifteen games over the Athletics. With seventy-one wins and only eight losses the team compiled a winning percentage of .899, which has never been approached by a professional baseball team since.

PROBLEMS ABOUND IN NATIONAL ASSOCIATION

The early league had problems in addition to Boston's dominance. There was no minimum standard of play. Any team in the country willing to put up the ten dollar entry fee and throw up a temporary grandstand

11

could join. Some of the teams were so poor that they refused to go on the road, playing only at home and forfeiting the rest of their schedule. Many players felt no obligation to honor contracts and might show up at any park, wearing any uniform. Rules were loose, and enforcement of them was even looser. The rules committee had little authority to demand adherence to the regulations and seemed reluctant to exercise what power it did possess.

It was widely assumed that gambling was rampant. "Hippodroming," or throwing of games for a price, was openly discussed. The Boston team was an exception to the rule. No shady dealing by the players was tolerated, its park was sturdier and kept cleaner, and the owners kept their focus on building a consistent winner. Judging by the standings, the efforts paid off.

THE NATIONAL LEAGUE

In 1876 a decision was made by team owners to disband the association in favor of a more structured league, which they named the National League. The formal name reflected a shift in power. Where the original group was an association of professional baseball *players*, the new circuit was to be known as the National League of Professional Baseball *Clubs*. The owners were now in the driver's seat. The league was pared to the eight strongest teams, and future expansion was limited to cities over a certain size.

The Cincinnati team came back to life at that time, and in gentlemanly fashion the Boston club returned the name "Red Stockings" to them. After a series of informal name changes, Boston's baseball team became known as the Braves.

THE FIRST PROFESSIONAL LEAGUE

When baseball was still in its infancy many professional teams roamed the countryside playing games with anyone they could find. A championship team retained its title until beaten in a series with another squad.

In 1871 the NA, as the National Association was known, was chartered, and staged a season-long tournament for the title. It was a diffuse group with loose rules. Each team paid a ten-dollar entrance fee and had to arrange a best-of-five series with each of the other teams in the league. At the end of the season the wins were totaled and the champion earned the right to fly the "whip-pennant" over its stadium for the following year.

WHAT'S IN A NAME?

The team we most commonly call the Braves had many names. Initially it chose "Red Stockings," but gave that name back to Cincinnati when that team reconstituted itself. Boston then called itself, in succession: Red Caps, Reds, Beaneaters, Doves (after its owners, the Dovie Brothers), Rustlers (after its owner, John Russell), Braves, Bees, and back to Braves again. To avoid confusion, the team is referred to as the Boston Braves throughout that time frame.

Boston did not dominate in the new league as it had in the old one. Built on a foundation of strong teams, the new league's pennant race was taken more seriously. Although the Braves did not win the pennant in the first season, they came back strong in 1877 and 1878, and again in 1883. The next few years, however, were disappointing, and they fell into the lower half of the standings. In the off-season before 1888 the owners made several key decisions in an attempt to bring the team back to prominence. The first was to purchase the contract of Mike "King" Kelly, baseball's first true media star. He had previously caught for Chicago and his became a household name. The purchase price for Kelly was an unprecedented $10,000. (For a frame of reference, Jordan Marsh advertised tennis shoes that day for $2.50, and Wilmot's of Washington Street had all-wool suits for sale for as low as $8.)

Also coming from Chicago was Kelly's teammate, Massachusetts hero John Clarkson, born just across the Charles River from Boston, in Cambridge. And, adding further to the baseball excitement in Boston was the decision to rebuild the South End Grounds. It was the only stadium unchanged since the beginnings of the National Association, and it was time to build a park befitting the new talent.

THE GRAND PAVILION

The Grand Pavilion was a double-decked structure topped off with spires, capped with pennants flapping in the breeze. The main body on the first level was divided into nine sections, labeled "A" through "I," with 20 rows each, holding 2,028 patrons. At the front of section E was a press box for reporters and a telegraph operator. The balcony had an additional seven sections with eight rows each, totaling 778 seats. Attached to each end of the covered pavilion were open-air bleachers, with 1,300 seats for

13

KING KELLY

Baseball star Michael "King" Kelly was viewed as quite a ladies' man and was sought after for every party. He knew how to get publicity, and whether good or bad, he loved it. Legend says that one teammate had him followed by a private detective. According to a story called "Beer Drinkers and Hell Raisers," the detective reported back that Kelly had been seen "drinking lemonade" at 3 A.M. When confronted, King Kelly responded, "It was straight whiskey. I never drink lemonade at that hour."

King was colorful on the baseball diamond as well, constantly trying to steal bases. Whenever he made his attempts the crowd would urge him on, chanting, "Slide, Kelly, Slide!" His actions prompted artist Frank O. Small to paint a picture of Kelly sliding into second at the South End Grounds. In 1890 Mike Kelly joined up with the Brotherhood League, playing for and managing the new Boston entry. He finished his career in New York, and died four years later at age thirty-six, after having contracted pneumonia.

King Kelly himself claimed he was not the best runner, so he perfected the slide. An 1889 song by J. W. Kelly (no relation) became baseball's first popular ballad, poking fun at Kelly with this nonsensical chorus:

Slide, Kelly, slide!
Your running's a disgrace.
Slide, Kelly, Slide!
Stay there, hold your base.

For if someone doesn't steal you
Or your batting doesn't fail you,
They'll take you to Australia,
Slide, Kelly, slide!"

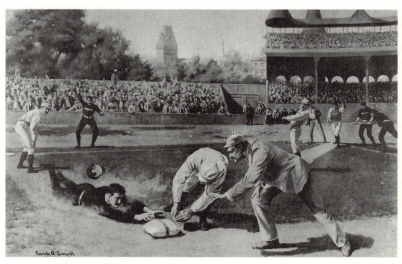

FIGURE 4: *Slide Kelly Slide*, showing the inside of the South End Grounds; painted by Frank O. Small, 1890. *Courtesy of Boston Public Library, Print Department*

each side. As with its predecessor on the same site, the pavilion backed up onto Walpole Street. From the outside it resembled a medieval castle or fairground; from the street four of the six main turrets, each reaching more than sixty feet into the sky, were clearly visible. Outside of the structure, and surrounding the park, was a wooden fence fifteen feet high. Tickets were sold from booths built into the fence. The main entrance, between the middle turrets, was ornate, bounded by columns on each side, fancy scrollwork across the top, and the word "Pavilion" directly over the doorway. By many accounts it was the grandest stadium in the country.

The feeling was not universal, however, as one *Globe* columnist spoke for another viewpoint. Giving the fans a boost, rather than the playing field, he said, "Perhaps there are many people in this country who do not believe that Boston is the greatest base ball city in the world. If those people could only have a bird's eye view of the Boston Grounds yesterday afternoon they would award the supremacy to the Hub." He went on, "5,400 people sitting in uncomfortable seats. Several hundred more standing on the damp ground with their hands down deep in their pockets, stamping and doing the best they could to keep warm wildly cheering."

Throughout the next few years the park was complimented on its architecture, but criticized for its lack of comfort and poor sight lines.

GRAND OPENING

April 11, 1894, opening day at the reconfigured park, was celebrated in ominous weather. As the place filled up, threatening clouds worried the owners as they worked the admission booth. By game time a light rain had developed, but it was not heavy enough for a postponement, which would mean a return of the gate receipts.

Among the public the grand opening was viewed as a civic occasion. Most politicians of the day attended. Even advertisements in the newspapers were slanted toward the big event of the day.

THE NEW PARK ABLAZE

As grand as the pavilion may have been, it was short-lived. At the end of the third inning of a game with Baltimore on May 15, 1894, disaster struck.

A fire started as a tiny flicker underneath the extreme right field bleachers at 4:10 P.M. As the Boston team made its last out of the inning and players headed for their positions, right fielder Jim "Foxy" Bannon

"THE GRAND STAND"

The base ball grounds will be filled on Friday and Saturday with an admiring audience. The players will be received with enthusiasm befitting their individual merits. The consciousness of being well and fittingly equipped is doubtless a support and inspiration to participants in any struggle. This suggests moral reflection. We are all desirous of appearing presently before some grandstand for some reason. Our grandstand is to arrive at perfection in the art of equipping everybody for everything.

This G. W. Simmons & Company's ad appeared just before the grand opening.

FIGURE 5: Grandstand of the South End Grounds, taken from Walpole Street; 1890. *Courtesy of Boston Public Library, Print Department*

spotted a small curl of smoke come up through the bleachers. Some of the fans noticed it as well, but did not take it seriously. Well-known Boston supporter General "Hi Hi" Dixwell joked with one of the owners that it was a "hot game today." (For more information on Dixwell, see pp. 134–35.) Bannon did not take it so lightly. He raced over to try and quell the small flame before it got out of hand. After trying desperately to stamp it out with his feet, he then resorted to using his cap to smother it. A sudden gust of wind roared across the park with a gale force. It hit the flame and transformed it into a wall of fire. Bannon then gave up and ran for help. A few moments later the whole section of right-field bleachers became a raging inferno. The famed Sullivan Tower, outside the park—often used by those wanting to see the game without paying the admission price—went next. The fire then spread to the wooden structures all along Berlin Street, just beyond the right-field fence.

At first those in the Grand Pavilion sat mesmerized by the fire. As the heat intensified, however, fans began to pour out of the park into the surrounding neighborhood. A few unlucky souls headed for the apparent safety of the infield, but a sudden twist of the firestorm's track put them in grave danger. There was a flash beneath the main structure behind home plate and the pavilion was completely engulfed just seconds after it had been evacuated. The fire then skirted along the low, wooden outer structure to the left-field bleachers. Within seconds a ring of fire nearly trapped those that had run to the middle of the park. For some inexplicable reason a small portion of the far-left-field fence was spared, and those trapped were able to escape to Camden and Gainsborough Streets. The heat became nearly unbearable, but all survived with only minor injuries. The fire continued to spread throughout the neighborhood, destroying belongings, accumulated over a lifetime, of all those who lived in the small wooden tenements around the ball field.

The fire marshal credited groundskeeper John Haggerty with keeping a cool head. Like Bannon, he too attempted to put the blaze out, but failed. He tried to convince a policeman on duty to call in the alarm, but in the confusion the officer did not do so. He then led many patrons to safety and ran to the nearest engine house himself to alert the fire department. The notification took place at 4:22 P.M., twelve minutes after Jim Bannon had first spotted the fire. Haggerty returned to a fully engulfed stadium; by then the fire had also claimed his own little house on Walpole Street, across from the park's entrance.

Within forty-five minutes the blaze destroyed the entire stadium as well as all structures on Walpole, Cunard, Coventry, and Burke Streets, and parts of Berlin and Tremont Streets. In all, four hundred thousand dollars' worth of damage was reported. Most of the value was in the stadium, as the insurance company assigned low assessments to the wooden residences.

How the Fire Began

Throughout the next few days several theories emerged as to how the fire started. According to the *Boston Globe*, the story that was eventually accepted by the fire marshal came from a fourteen-year-old street urchin named Jimmy Lasky, who lived at 4 Seneca Street, by the Fort Point

Channel. He related his version to Boston second baseman Bobby Lowe, and later to Fire Marshal John Flynn. After the first inning ended he and two friends, who were outside the park, made their way through the crowd that was hanging around the entrance to the 25-cent bleachers. He scouted along the fence to find one of several spots he had apparently burrowed for the purpose of sneaking into the game. He chose an entrance farthest from the policeman on duty (*Boston Globe*, May 16, 1894).

He told Flynn, "Us fellers never pay to get in and are on to all the places."

After getting past the outer perimeter he jumped onto a shed, and from there over to the next fence. He climbed down the other side and crawled under the bleachers. There he found a hole to slip into where he could watch the game unimpeded. Directly above him a man took out a cigar and match. At first Jimmy considered asking the man if he had another cigar for him, but the batter hit the ball and everyone in the stands above Lasky jumped to their feet. Apparently either the cigar or lit match dropped down below the bleachers. At first Jimmy thought nothing of it, but he started getting warm; he looked around and saw the blaze. After trying to put it out, he decided that he and his friends had better get out while they could. He ran to a policeman and gave a detailed description of the man with the cigar, but the patrolman apparently did not take him seriously.

FIGURE 6: Burning of the South End Grounds, from the rear of the park, May 15, 1894. *Reprinted courtesy of* The Boston Globe

FIRE DAMAGE

The park blaze did considerable damage. In all, twelve acres had been scorched, 190 dwellings were destroyed, and 1,900 people were left homeless. Before the day was over, the stadium, a school, and an engine house were reduced to ashes and rubble. Baseball hardly missed a beat. The team owners contracted to use the Congress Street Grounds—abandoned home of the former American Association team—for a month while the South End field was rebuilt. The fire-shortened game was replayed the next day. (For more information on the Congress Street Grounds, see chapter 11.)

Upon further investigation the fire marshal concluded that the boy's story was true. During the winter some of the center-field bleachers had been removed due to rotting. The workers had left piles of sawdust beneath the remaining right-field seats; the cigar or match probably landed in the pile and ignited. The fierce wind fanned the flames until they were out of control.

Amazingly, despite the extensive damage, no one was killed or seriously hurt. For two days after the fire, people believed that Jimmy Lasky had been a victim, as he could not be found. When he reappeared and was asked where he had been, he explained that he had gotten very dirty from the fire and was afraid to go home, for fear of "getting in trouble."

THE PARK REOPENS JUNE 20, 1894

In little over a month the team returned to the third incarnation of the South End field. Because the original structure had not been fully insured the replacement was smaller and much less ornate than the Grand Pavilion. The main grandstand had a seating capacity of 900. There were more outside bleacher seats, however, making up most of the difference. Although not as impressive as the old building, the new park had more comfortable seating and better sight lines. The reopening was marked by an appearance of St. Augustine's Cadet Band, which played an appropriate piece for each player as he was introduced. The fans that day—5,206 people, including 100 standing-room ticket holders—watched as Boston demolished the New York nine 12 to 1.

SOCCER'S FIRST TRY

Later in 1894 the first attempt at professional soccer was hosted at the rebuilt sports palace. The six eastern teams of baseball's National League formed the American League of Professional Football [Soccer] Clubs. The purpose was to introduce a new sport to the baseball crowd and to make more efficient use of the home grounds. The schedules were written so that the soccer teams used the fields when the baseball teams were away, and vice versa. Boston's Beaneaters played teams from New York, Philadelphia, Brooklyn, Baltimore, and Washington.

But the league was ill conceived. According to the late Sam Foulds, former historian of the United States Soccer Federation, little thought was put into the operation. For instance, the baseball manager also served as the soccer manager. Two problems immediately arose. First, baseball managers generally knew nothing about soccer. And second, in the event that they did know something about the game, they would be out of town with the baseball team when the soccer games were played. One exception to this arrangement took place in Baltimore, where a knowledgeable soccer coach was hired. That club's foresight caused a further problem for the league, as Baltimore ran away with the title: there was little interest at any stadium unless Baltimore was the opposition. The league only lasted the one season.

BASEBALL PLAY-OFFS: THE TEMPLE CUP TOURNAMENT

Before 1892, the year that the American Association disbanded, a predecessor to the modern World Series had taken place. (For more information on the American Association, see pp. 130–31, 141–42.) This attempt to have a title series ended when baseball was again reduced to one major league, leaving a post-season void. In 1894 another effort was made to add the excitement of a play-off into the sport. Beginning that year the Temple Cup Tournament, a best-of-seven series, was played, matching the pennant winner against the second-place team. Although some interest was generated, most fans viewed the pennant winner as the true champion regardless of the outcome.

Boston was only involved in the tournament once. In 1897 the Braves finished first, thus pitting them against the second-place Baltimore Orioles. Game one was played at the South End on October 4. A large assembly was on hand to see what was destined to be the only game Boston ever won in the series: 9,600 fans arrived to see the Braves, who dominated the Orioles in the regular season, once again beat back the team from Baltimore. The bleachers were packed to the limit an

AN ENDLESS BORE

Of the first game in the Temple Cup Tournament, the *Boston Post* wrote, "The moon was high, the stars were out. The hush of evening had come down. 10,000 strove to distinguish the Bostons and the Baltimores in the gloom." The fans wanted the game called on account of darkness but the umpire insisted it continue. Apparently the league was in no mood to reschedule a game when it was already very late in the season.

The fans, or "cranks" as they were known then, yelled, "Call the game!" The umpire yelled back, "Play it out!" while swatting at gnats. The *Post* continued, "Jennings hit one somewhere over first base and went to second, and Keeler to third, while the ball was being found. Kelly hit to Long and was out at first which was practically a gift to Boston, otherwise they might have played all night" (October 5, 1897).

hour before game time; in front of the bleachers extra seats were added. Unfortunately, by most accounts the game was a seemingly endless bore, and continued well beyond dusk. The Braves won the game 13–12.

Game two, also played at Boston, saw a crowd of sixty-five hundred with Baltimore victorious 13–11. Game three, the last one in Boston, had an attendance of five thousand, as the crowds continued to dwindle. Boston lost 8–3 in a game called in the eighth inning. The series moved to Baltimore, where there was even less interest. Game four had an attendance of twenty-five hundred, and the final match was seen by only seven hundred paying fans. Baltimore won the series four games to one, and the Temple Cup Tournament was never played again.

THE BRAVES SINK

As the twentieth century dawned, the Boston Braves had lost much of their luster, sinking lower in the standings each year. By 1906 they had reached the bottom, and beginning in 1909 they started a four-year stay in the cellar. Adding to their on-field problems, time seemed to have bypassed the club. Their stadium was now woefully out of date. Even the crosstown rival Red Sox had moved from their Huntington Avenue home to spacious quarters in the modern Fenway Park. The South End Grounds was now the oldest, and by far the smallest, park in the nation. In 1913 the Braves clawed their way back up to fifth place, but at thirty-two games off the mark they were still much closer to the bottom than the top. Even the purchase of the team by real-estate magnate James Gaffney had not shaken off the doldrums.

The Braves began the 1914 season no differently. On the Fourth of July, with more than two months of the schedule completed, the Boston Braves sat at the bottom of the standings once again. The oldest continuously operated professional baseball team, with its glorious past, had become a ghost of its former self.

A MIRACLE HAPPENS

The team put on a show for the ages; they began beating everyone. Through the months of July and August they climbed higher and higher in the standings, and the crowds began shifting their attention from the highly touted Red Sox, who had a strong chance at the American League flag, to the once-lowly Braves, who seemed to be doing the impossible. Everyone, including their crosstown rival, got caught up in the excitement. When the South End Grounds began bursting at the seams, Joseph Lannin, president of the Red Sox, offered them the use of his much bigger Fenway Park. At first James Gaffney of the Braves accepted the offer only for Saturday games. On August 1 the Braves played their first "home" game at the American League park, and returned to the South End during the week. The attendance at Fenway was twenty thousand, which far exceeded their average tightly packed seventy-five hundred at home. The following Saturday saw a return to Fenway, where the crowd reached fourteen thousand.

During the next week the Braves played for the final time in the last remaining park from 1871. On Monday, August 10, 1914, eighty-five hundred witnessed this piece of history as the Braves beat Cincinnati 3 to 1. (On Tuesday the teams did play again, but the game ended in a 0 to 0 tie when called in the thirteenth inning, therefore being wiped from the record books.) Rain canceled the Wednesday game and the team took off on an extended road trip. When it returned on September 7, it moved the rest of its season to Fenway, ending the baseball life of the legendary park by the side of the tracks.

The Boston Braves continued their incredible run; they won the National League Pennant and took the Athletics in the World Series in four straight games. The home games of the series were played at Fenway. They began the following year at Fenway Park, but closed out the season at brand-new Braves Field on Commonwealth Avenue. (For more information on Braves Field, see chapter 4.)

SOCCER BRINGS NEW LIFE TO THE PARK

The old field had not quite died, however; new life was breathed into it during the Roaring Twenties. In 1921, nearby Northeastern University played its baseball games there. In the same year the American Soccer League formed along the eastern seaboard. The teams were owned mostly by such large companies as Bethlehem Steel, Indiana Flooring, and in Andover, Massachusetts, twenty miles north of Boston, the American Woolen Company. (For more information on the Andover team, see chapter 14.) Soccer began building a reputation, placing it second to baseball in the consciousness of American sports enthusiasts.

In 1924 G. A. G. Wood formed the Boston Soccer Club. The new entrant stirred things up. Gate receipts for the entire league that year doubled from the year before. The team's president, Wood, said, "We spent a lot of money because we realized that nothing was too good for the Hub." Wherever the team traveled, fans came out to see the Wonder Workers—the name was unofficial but, according to contemporary reports, well deserved. Aside from Billy Gonsalves, the team had a decided Scottish flair. Most of the players were either born in Scotland or had Scottish ancestry. Gonsalves was born in Fall River and played for two years in Boston. He moved home, playing for the Fall River Marksmen, then moved with them to New York. (For more information on Fall River, see chapter 13.) Barney Battles was born in Scotland, but moved to the United States as a young boy. He played for the Wonder Workers through the 1928 season, before signing with a team in the Scottish League, where he finished his career. Playing on the forward line, both Battles and Gonsalves were solid goal scorers.

After several years of neglect the field, which became known as the Walpole Street Grounds, was in rough shape. On dry days the ground was too hard for good play. On rainy days the players could be ankle deep in mud. Like an aging movie star, though, the ancient field bestowed a certain big-time status on its tenants. Thousands of Boston fans took

WONDER WORKERS AND WOODSIES

The official name of the team was a very generic-sounding Boston Soccer Club, but the club earned a couple of nicknames that took hold. In the early days newspaper reporters called them the "Woodsies" in honor of their owner, G. A. G. Wood. Later the name "Wonder Workers" became dominant and stuck with the club until the end.

to the team, whose members wore blue shorts and gold shirts (with a large blue "B" emblazoned on the front). The Wonder Workers were extremely successful at home, not losing their first game there until four months into the season.

LEWIS CUP TOURNAMENT

In its first year the team did well enough as an expansion club to finish fourth in the twelve-team league, behind such perennial powerhouses as Fall River, Bethlehem Steel, and Brooklyn. In addition to the league championship the ASL, a predominantly east-coast operation, also operated a tournament for the Lewis Cup. This trophy was copped by the Wonder Workers.

The ancient but fading St. Louis Professional Soccer League, in an attempt to position itself as the western version of the American League, challenged the Boston team to play its own trophy winner in a best-of-three contest for the American Professional Championship. The American League, secure in its knowledge that it was the premier circuit in the nation, accepted the challenge. The first game was played in St. Louis where the local Ben Millers upset the Wonder Workers. Determined to end with victory, Boston easily outclassed the St. Louis group when the teams returned to Walpole Street, in front of four thousand supportive fans. Boston finished off the series in St. Louis, earning the team a trip to the White House to meet with President Coolidge.

Soccer had become so popular that a minor league team began play, joining the Wonder Workers at Walpole Street the following year. The Hubs, playing in the National League, lasted only the one season, however. (Despite its name, the National League played almost exclusively in New England, yet had a reputation second only to the American League.)

The major league Wonder Workers continued their winning ways, taking the Lewis Cup again in 1927, and later surprising the Uruguay National Team, Olympic gold medalists, and soon-to-be World Cup winners, beating them 2 to 1. (See pp. 189–90 for more information on that game.) In 1928 the team lost the Lewis Cup in the final game of the tournament, but did manage to win the league championship later that season. The team attracted world attention, enabling it to host the famed Glasgow Celtics, whom they held to a 2-to-2 draw.

WALPOLE STREET GROUNDS PASSING

The Wonder Workers seemed destined to join the ranks of Boston's permanent sports scene, rubbing elbows with the Braves, Red Sox, and the brand-new Bruins, until an event happened that seemed to break the spell. Buried on page 22 of the *Boston Globe* was an article that not only signaled the team's downward spiral, but it very quietly announced that the curtain was dropping on an important part of Boston's sports legacy. The small headline halfway down the page of the February 10, 1929, edition proclaimed "Walpole Street Grounds Passing." The subheading said, "Soccer Games Will Be Played Elsewhere." It went on to say that the stadium site was to be taken back by the New York, New Haven, & Hartford Railroad. In just eighty-seven words the end was announced for the old South End Grounds, the last remaining park dating itself back to the very beginning of professional sports leagues.

In the last game of any type ever played on the storied ground, the Boston Wonder Workers lost to the Newark Skeeters 4 to 3. George M. Collins of the *Boston Globe* said that the major upset was played on a "heavy field, ankle deep in mud."

As the field reverted back to its former life as a railroad yard, the Wonder Workers moved on, trying to regroup. The soccer club scheduled its future games at the high-school stadium in Everett, but the magic of the early years was gone. The team lasted only another year. As the Great Depression set in, the large industrial firms no longer had the resources to support such endeavors, and by 1932 the entire league was in deep financial trouble.

The site of the old South End Grounds today shows no signs of its past career, when it served as an integral part of Boston's sports life. In 1938 the Armour Meat Packing Company moved in, wiping out most signs of the stadium. By the 1970s Armour was gone and the area had become an undeveloped parking lot for Northeastern University. For a

---

PENNANT UPS AND DOWNS

In the spring of 1884, Boston's National League baseball team, the Braves, was celebrating its championship of the year before. A new flagpole had been erected in center field to prominently display the new pennant. With the words "League Champions—1883" emblazoned on the bunting, the pennant was raised up the pole to warm applause. As it reached the top it was unfurled for all to see that the words were upside down. The applause turned to snickering, and then to gales of laughter and derision, as the poor linesman clumsily pulled the flag down in order to put it right.

time, street signs and curbing still remained as ghosts of Walpole and Grinnell Streets, providing a rough perimeter of the old stadium. Today even those are gone. A visitor to the area will now find the Ruggles Street station of the rapid transit system and Northeastern's modern parking garage occupying the spot where Boston's professional sports history began.

OPENED: May 8, 1901

CLOSED: October 7, 1911

FIELD MEASUREMENTS:

Original	*1908 changes*
Left field 350 feet	
Deep center field 530 feet	Deep center field 635 feet
Right field 280 feet	Right field 320 feet

CAPACITY: 9,000 to 11,500

TENANTS:

Boston Red Sox (American League); *baseball, 1901 to 1911*

The Boston Red Sox have been playing at Fenway Park for so long it is now hard to imagine them anywhere else. Their current field, with all its quirks and corners, is as much a part of their heritage as Ted Williams, Carl Yastrzemski, and Tom Yawkey. Their original home is nearly forgotten. As a new century opened a new baseball league, a new team, and a new park sprang up literally in the shadows of the Braves, one of the National League's legendary members. The upstart Red Sox immediately eclipsed the Braves, and ultimately extinguished them from the New England sports scene. The Boston Red Sox attained legendary status in their first home, but as Fenway Park lives on as the oldest stadium in baseball, memories of the Huntington Avenue Grounds, where the Red Sox made baseball history, have been relegated to the dusty back corners of the team's archives.

Huntington Avenue is called the "Avenue of the Arts" and began developing that reputation long ago. The neighborhood is, or has been, home to the Boston Symphony Orchestra, the Opera House, the Museum of Fine Arts, and the Massachusetts Horticultural Society. The New England Manufacturing and Mechanical Institute, a combination museum and exhibition hall, once stood there; the structure covered ten acres and was thought to be the largest of its kind in the world. It was destroyed in a massive fire on June 22, 1886, resulting in seven deaths.

When the remnants of that building were knocked down the area was dubbed the Huntington Carnival Lot, hosting traveling circuses and shows, and sporting a permanent Chute-the-Shoots flume ride. As the traveling circuses moved to larger space in Charlestown, at the other end of the city, the land filled with railroad yards, giving no hint that it was destined to take part in a baseball revolution brewing against the monopolistic National League.

A NEW LEAGUE

Ban Johnson, president of the minor Western League, was intent on making a mark in the world of sports. In late 1899 he announced that his organization would change its name to the American League and attain major status by 1901. His plan was to replace seven of the teams in small, midwestern cities by creating new ones in large metropolises. Initially he had felt it best to try to avoid an outright war with the older,

(overleaf) FIGURE 7: Airplane view of the baseball field at Huntington Avenue; 1911.

Courtesy of Boston Public Library, Print Department

established league, opting to stay away from most of its cities. Boston had always been a risky place to contest the NL head-on; two upstart leagues had already tried and failed.

Despite Johnson's concessions, the National League did not take the threat lightly. It announced the creation of a new American Association, to serve as a sister league to its own—the plan was to field teams in many of the proposed American League cities. For good measure a team was planned for the Boston area as well, which would play its games on the Cambridge side of the Charles River. The sole purpose of the new association seemed to be to thwart Johnson's efforts.

A NEW TEAM FOR BOSTON

With the gauntlet thrown down, Johnson counterattacked. Scouts were sent to Boston to seek out potential sites for a new American League ballpark, resulting in a signed lease for the Huntington Carnival Lot. A meeting was held at the Grand Pacific Hotel in Chicago in January to finalize plans. The *Boston Herald* reported, "With a business-like punctuality not characteristic of their major rivals [the NL] the American League magnates convened on time and spent the afternoon hard at work." Abandoning all plans to bypass cities with NL teams, the American League decided to go head-to-head with the older league, putting teams in the National League strongholds of Boston, Philadelphia, and Chicago. During the meeting a ten-year agreement was reached. Leases, stock options, and franchises were awarded, and the AL placed teams in Boston, Philadelphia, Baltimore, Washington, Cleveland, Detroit, Chicago, and Milwaukee.

THE NATIONAL LEAGUE FIGHTS BACK

The National League tried to head off defections to the new league. Hugh Duffy, a well-regarded player for Boston's National League Braves, was offered the job as player-manager with its proposed sister team, planned for Cambridge. He had already decided, though, to make the jump with Ban Johnson, and would not back down. He declared in no uncertain terms to the press, "I am with the American League" (*Boston Herald*, January 29, 1901). He was an important catch for the new enterprise. In 1894, while playing in Boston for the National League, Hugh Duffy batted a league-leading .438, a record to this day.

He later made stronger remarks concerning the proposed job offer in Cambridge. They "will not make a go of the new American Association club near Boston, for the grounds are too far out," he declared. "They are in Cambridge and will not draw from Boston. Harvard students might patronize the club, but that is about all."

The war of words between the established National League and the new American circuit continued to heat up. Officials of the older league announced in the *Boston Herald*, "We will not make an attempt at conflicting schedules. We will do what we please and let the American League do likewise" (January 29, 1901).

Rumors that a truce had been arranged between the rival circuits were building. The prevailing story was that as a gesture of goodwill the American League was ready to drop Boston from the lineup, thus leaving the city to the Braves. If that were true the league would probably look to Louisville or Indianapolis as a replacement. Red Sox owner Charles Somers made it absolutely clear that Boston was indeed represented in the American League in 1901, telling *Herald* reporters, "It is amusing to note how difficult it is for some people to digest our proposition. You are at liberty to say that we stand as firm as Gibraltar. We gave the NL plenty of opportunity to talk the situation over. The time for such concession is past. Boston will have a place in the American League under any circumstance" (*Boston Herald*, February 21, 1901).

A NEW PARK

Groundbreaking for the new park came on the cold and windy morning of March 7, 1901. The proceedings began with the raising of Old Glory at the park's proposed entrance. All guests then paraded to the center of the empty lot where fan extraordinaire Arthur Dixwell took the first shovelful of dirt from the ground. (For more information on Dixwell, see pp. 134–35.) M. J. Moore, Hugh Duffy's brother-in-law, presided over the ceremony; looking on were many notables, including

---

WHAT'S IN A NAME?

At first the Red Sox simply called themselves the "Americans," to differentiate themselves from the crosstown "Nationals." Sportswriters tried on many nicknames, starting with Pilgrims, followed by Puritans, Somersets (after owner Charlie Somers), and Plymouth Rocks. In 1908 they harkened back to early Boston baseball history and began calling themselves the "Red Sox." The last name stuck. An outline of a red sock was placed on the front of the uniforms, forming possibly the first team logo.

FIGURE 8: The crowd watches a boy climb over the wall at the Huntington Avenue Grounds, ca. 1904. *Courtesy of Boston Public Library, Print Department; creator, Edmunds E. Bond*

Michael J. Sullivan, a former well-known player who had since become a Boston attorney. Following the events of the morning the entire crowd, consisting of one hundred invited guests and about one hundred others, were entertained with a lunch, where toasts were made honoring the new team, new league, and brand-new stadium. The assembled gathering, all shivering in the wind despite heavy jackets and derbies, were happy to get in out of the cold. They joked that the outfield would be so large, no one would ever hit one over the fence.

The Huntington Avenue park was bounded on the northwest by Huntington Avenue, directly across the street from the Boston Storage building. The Opera House could be seen clearly over the left-field wall. On the southwest was Rogers Street, today's Forsyth Street. To the immediate east were the railroad yards of the New York, New Haven, & Hartford line. Just beyond the tracks was the South End Grounds, fabled home of the Boston National League franchise since 1871.

Construction crews completed their work in early May. The grandstand sat on the southern end of the property, facing north. With one entrance on the southwest corner of the grandstand on Rogers Street, the main entrance was on the corner of Rogers and Huntington Avenue.

The main stands were of simple design, shaped as a semicircle. The room below the seats was divided into three sections. A covered lobby with a concrete floor fifteen feet wide ran the entire three hundred feet across the street side. The room to the left of the lobby held a concession stand; next to it was the box office, and on the extreme right of this section sat the director's office and a small private office. The center section contained room for patrons to park bicycles. The right section held locker rooms for both home and visiting squads, well equipped with lockers and shower facilities; men's and women's toilets; and space for the press.

The structure was built with expanded metal and roughcast cement, with a light gray tone. The roof rested on columns twenty-eight feet in the air, hipped on all four sides. The *Boston Globe* said it was "covered with granite felting, toned to a soft crimson" (February 22, 1901). Five flagpoles adorned the peaks, and archways at the back of the grandstand allowed a good light to reach the seating area. The interior was all-pine finish, and the floors were of rift hard pine. At each end of the grandstand was a set of bleachers. The structure, with its amenities, was considered a great improvement over the nearby National League grounds.

THE FIRST MANAGER

As the day for the opening pitch approached, the city came alive with anticipation. Daily, excited fans posed questions as to which players would be coming and—most important to the fans—who the new

---

BOTH PLAYER AND MANAGER

Today when the Boston Red Sox change managers the public interest generated is at least equal to that of choosing a new mayor. The situation was no different at the team's birth. The nod went to well-known third baseman for the Boston Braves, Jimmy Collins. He had been plying his baseball trade at the South End Grounds since 1895, but jumped to the new team and league when offered the chance to manage as well as to play. Continuing in his role at third base, Collins took over the duties of building a contender. He remained at the helm through 1906—a tenure surpassed only once in the team's history.

Playing in the field, he finished his career in Philadelphia with a lifetime batting average of .294.

manager would be. In early March, it became official: Jimmy Collins would play with and manage the new team. In his opening press conference Collins added to the war of words: "There is enough room for two teams in Boston providing there is no clash of dates" (*Boston Globe*, March 11, 1901). Sounding like Captain Parker on Lexington Green, he went on, "The American League is not looking for a fight, but is prepared if one is forced on them." He also said he had originally expected to be joining the new Buffalo club, but was happy to be in Boston. A reporter asked if this was a preference in cities, or was he happy because his bride-to-be lived in Massachusetts. He just smiled.

OPENING DAY, WEDNESDAY, MAY 8, 1901

Opening day at Huntington Avenue arrived and Boston became a two-baseball-team town. There was no time for a parade. The team arrived at Back Bay station at 2 P.M., game time. The road trip had not gone well, and they arrived at their new home with a 5–5 record. They were quickly transported down to the new park, which was decked out in flowers. All seats had been sold well in advance. The field had been advertised with a capacity of 9,000 but 10,500 baseball-mad Bostonians held passes. A local college professor, Charles Green, got into the spirit of the day. He handed small American flags to ticket holders as they entered the grounds; throughout the game the waving flags gave a nice effect. The *Boston Globe* reported, "It was a regular holiday attendance and the peanut man was in high glee as he sailed his paper bags among the joyous throngs in the bleachers."

Before the game started a special welcome was extended to the well-known players who had come over from the National League. Principal among them were the two player managers, Jimmy Collins of Boston and Nap LaJoie of the visiting Philadelphians. Both men got heroes' welcomes. Next, flowers were brought to home plate. A wreath of roses, with the word "Success" written in gold across the middle, was followed by a horseshoe of jonquils. The Boston owner, Charles Somers, was "happy with the Boston weatherman for furnishing such perfect conditions." Next came a line of carriages, parading through the center-field gate and across to the infield. They contained many old-time players. A new innovation, the "megaphone man," announced player changes and other interesting facts that the crowd wanted to hear.

Finally the players were introduced. First came the Philadelphia team, which received warm applause. Next came the Red Sox. The place erupted as the new American League contingent was welcomed into the

33

minds and hearts of the locals as if they had existed forever. Well-known fan General Arthur "Hi Hi" Dixwell was given the honor of tossing out the first ball, and the game was underway. (For more information on Dixwell, see pp. 134–35.)

Although a party atmosphere reigned for the entire afternoon, the game itself was an anticlimax. It was a walkover for the Red Sox almost from the first inning. Cy Young, already a legend, mowed down the opposition, allowing only a couple of scattered hits. He eased up after the seventh inning in order to rest his arm. The game ended with Boston on top 12–4. The teams would play again the next day, and Philadelphia owner Connie Mack promised he would wake his team up before that.

On June 17 the American League Red Sox got their initial test of drawing power as the date marked the first time that they would be in town together with the National League Braves, across the tracks at the South End Grounds. The new team had the nicer park, with a twenty-five-cent admission. The Braves charged double, but had habit and tradition on their side. In a Bunker Hill Day double-header the new team fared quite well. In the first game it drew 5,000 spectators, and 10,000 in the second; the National League team could only muster up 1,500 fans. On June 18 the Braves cut their admission price in half, but the pattern continued throughout the life of the Huntington Avenue Grounds. In each of the first years that the teams coexisted, the Red Sox outdrew the Braves. In that inaugural year the difference was 289,000 to 146,000. Chicago, which also had two teams, showed the same result, with the American League team on top. In Philadelphia the two leagues drew about the same-sized audience.

The Red Sox not only drew new fans to the game, they also siphoned off many once loyal to the Braves. Chief among them were the Royal Rooters and their leader, the Grand Exalted Ruler of Rooters Row, Michael "Nuf Ced" McGreevey. As ticket prices at the South End Grounds rose, interest among the Royal Rooters began to wane. With the new American League team and its stadium nearby, the Rooters switched allegiances and began cheering on the new hometown boys.

Wherever the Red Sox went, so did the Royal Rooters, led by saloon keeper McGreevey. He and his customers filled whole sections of the Huntington Avenue Grounds on as many occasions as was practical. The group at times followed the Red Sox to other cities for "away" games, determined to make as much noise as possible, thus giving the Red Sox some semblance of a home-field advantage. McGreevey passed out cards to the stalwarts, printed with chants which were often directed toward the

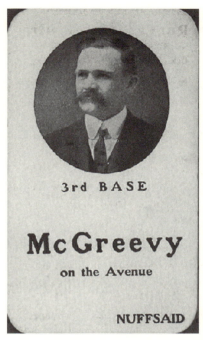
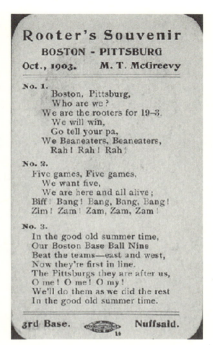

3rd BASE

McGreevy

on the Avenue

NUFFSAID

Rooter's Souvenir
BOSTON - PITTSBURG
Oct., 1903.   M. T. McGreevy

No. 1.
Boston, Pittsburg,
Who are we?
We are the rooters for 19-3.
We will win,
Go tell your pa,
We Beaneaters, Beaneaters,
Rah! Rah! Rah!

No. 2.
Five games, Five games,
We want five,
We are here and all alive;
Biff! Bang! Bang, Bang, Bang!
Zim! Zam! Zam, Zam, Zam!

No. 3.
In the good old summer time,
Our Boston Base Ball Nine
Beat the teams—east and west,
Now they're first in line.
The Pittsburgs they are after us,
O me! O me! O my!
We'll do them as we did the rest
In the good old summer time.

3rd Base.   Nuffsaid.

FIGURE 9: Royal Rooters souvenir card, with an advertisement for McGreevey's saloon, printed for the 1903 World Series. *Courtesy of Boston Public Library, Print Department*

opposition of the day. The idea was to get a whole section of the "foreign" stadium rooting for Boston, all from the same page. Of course, the back side of the cards contained advertisements for McGreevey's Third Base Saloon.

A FALL CLASSIC IS BORN

In 1903 the baseball war ended. The American Association—the National League's initial response to the threat to its monopoly—had not materialized. The American League had had a successful start, representing the model of stability in a business that is historically unstable. Through the first three years of operation not one team had been lost, and only two had moved to a new city. Not even the rock-solid National League could claim such a record. For the common good, both leagues opted for coexistence.

In a harkening back to the 1880s, the Boston Red Sox and the pennant-winning Pittsburgh Pirates of the National League agreed to meet in a best-of-nine series to determine the national championship. Some of the 35 older National League stalwarts grumbled, but the plans went forward. The first game of the series, and thus the first modern World Series game ever played, took place at the field on Huntington Avenue.

The agreement called for the first three games to be played in Boston. The following four (or as many of the four as might be necessary) would be in Pittsburgh. The two teams would then return to Boston. A crowd in excess of sixteen thousand was on hand for the beginning of this October tradition. In the first game Pittsburgh showed the superiority of the senior circuit, beating the home-ground favorites by a score of 7 to 3; Cy Young was the loser. After three games, Pittsburgh leading two games to one, the teams headed for western Pennsylvania to continue the series. As went the Red Sox, so did the Royal Rooters, intent on letting the Red Sox know that they had support from back home.

On October 6 Boston went down three games to one and things looked bleak, but the Royal Rooters were relentless. Every day they would go to Exposition Park and sing "Tessie," the club theme song, until they were hoarse. In the fifth game, behind ace Cy Young, Boston won, and the next day pitcher Bill Dineen tied the series at three and

---

NUF CED'S

In the 1890s Michael "Nuf Ced" McGreevey opened a liquor store at 940 Columbus Avenue in Boston. It became a "clubhouse" for players and fans alike. Everyone who knew baseball or wanted to know baseball would show up at McGreevey's before and after the games. As McGreevey's fame grew, so did his business, and eventually he opened a full bar and restaurant a few blocks away at 1153 Tremont Street. The official name was the Third Base Saloon, advertised as the "last place before going home." Most people called it "Nuf Ced's" (sometimes spelled Nuffsaid), after McGreevey's popular nickname. Michael McGreevey considered him-

self the ultimate resource on Boston baseball and ended all arguments by stating "Nuf Ced."

His saloon had light globes in the shape of baseballs, suspended on bats donated by such notable players and bar patrons as Cy Young, Freddie Parent, Nap LaJoie, Chuck Freeman, and Michael "King" Kelly. The grandfather clock in the corner had a bat for a pendulum. Standing guard over the outside doorway was the "Baseball Man," a life-sized dummy wearing a baseball uniform and holding a bat at his side. The bar is long gone, and, like the two nearby baseball parks it served, the site is part of the Northeastern University campus.

FIGURE 10: Interior view of McGreevey's Third Base Saloon, "The last place before going home," ca. 1910. Nuf Ced McGreevey was the leader of a band of rabid baseball fans, known as the Royal Rooters. *Courtesy of Boston Public Library, Print Department*

FIGURE 11: Exterior of McGreevey's Saloon, ca. 1910. The site today is part of the Northeastern University campus. *Courtesy of Boston Public Library, Print Department*

FIGURE 12: Fans on the field before game three of the 1903 World Series, October 3, 1903. *Courtesy of Boston Public Library, Print Department*

three. On October 10 in Pittsburgh, Boston took the lead, again winning behind Young. Back at Huntington Avenue, with the Red Sox holding a four-games-to-three advantage and needing only one more victory for the first world title, the Rooters were out in full force. To the odd strains of "Tessie, you're my only, only, only," the Boston Red Sox shut out and shut down the National League pennant winners. Boston had taken the first World Series, but more importantly, on that Tuesday afternoon at the Huntington Avenue Grounds, the American League could fully claim major league status.

THE TOP PITCHERS DUEL

Some of the greatest pitching duels in the sport took place at Huntington Avenue between the Boston Red Sox and the Philadelphia Athletics. Each team had on its staff some of the best hurlers baseball had seen. For Boston it was Cy Young. From Philadelphia came Rube Waddell, an eccentric who was lax about training and discipline but somehow managed to overpower the opposition more often than not. Legends were built around his antics. When it was discovered he was still married to his first wife—after he had married his second—he said he simply forgot to get divorced. Apparently he once saved a man from drowning; the story spread to the point where nine different people claimed to have been the near-victim.

Throughout the first decade of the twentieth century, debates raged

38

THE STORY OF TESSIE

From 1903 and extending through much of the twentieth century, the Red Sox had an unusual theme song called "Tessie." The music and lyrics have nothing to do with either baseball or Boston. Although stories and legends developed as to its origins, Nuf Ced McGreevey's own scrapbook appears to reveal the answer to the mystery.

In 1903 the American League pennant winners from Boston were scheduled to play Pittsburgh in the first "modern" World Series. To support the team both home and away McGreevey and his Royal Rooters planned a road trip. McGreevey wanted to bring a brass band with him to Pittsburgh, but costs prevented it. Instead the Rooters brought a big drum and noisemakers and sent club member and piano player Tom Burton to find a theme song. His orders were to find something modern, popular, and cheap. He opted for a tune called "Tessie," written by Will R. Anderson and featured in John C. Fisher's musical, *The Silver Slipper*. It had not been a big hit and had passed its prime, but the price was right. He went back to McGreevey and the Royal Rooters, who gave unanimous approval for Burton to go the frugal route. The song became the team's theme song. It was still being played on opening days at Fenway Park well into the 1960s by organist John Kiley.

TESSIE

Tessie, you make me feel so badly.
Why don't you turn around?
Tessie you know I love you madly.
Babe, my heart weighs about a pound.
Don't blame me if I ever doubt you.
You know I couldn't live without you.
Tessie, you are my only, only, only.

---

over who was the superior pitcher, Young or Waddell. Although Cy Young was the hometown favorite, Waddell was also very popular in Boston, bringing out a formidable crowd each time he visited Huntington.

The showdown came during a two-week period in 1904 when some of the greatest pitching ever witnessed took place. The series of match-ups started on April 25, when the two men met in Philadelphia. Both pitchers were throwing well, but Waddell came out on top, 2–0. His victory, although well deserved, was aided by the poor fielding of Boston. Cy Young gave up only two runs, and none after the first inning, but his team committed six errors. Although Young pitched well, without an offense the best he could have hoped for was a 0–0 draw. In the last two innings he did not give up a hit, beginning an incredible streak that lasted until May 11.

THE CYCLONE

"Cyclone" is how his contemporaries described Denton True Young's fastball, and that is how one of the best pitchers ever, earned the name "Cy." An Ohio native, he split most of his spectacular career between Cleveland and Boston, playing for two teams in each city. By the time he retired, he had notched an incredible 511 wins, nearly 100 more than his closest rival.

After playing with Cleveland's National League club for eight seasons and a brief stint in St. Louis, he joined the American League in its inaugural season, playing in Boston at the Huntington Avenue Grounds. He reached his peak there, winning at least twenty games in all but one of his eight seasons with the club. Twice he reached the thirty-game plateau. On May 5, 1904, he stunned the baseball world by tossing the first "modern" perfect game, which was also the second of his three no-hitters. In fact, until Hideo Nomo's gem for the 2001 Red Sox, Young stood as the only pitcher to hurl no-hitters in two different centuries.

In 1909 Cy Young returned to Cleveland, playing for the American League entry, but then came back to Boston, for the National League Braves this time. His name is immortalized by the Cy Young Award, presented to baseball's best pitcher each year.

On April 30, as Boston was playing the winless Senators, Captain Collins decided to put young George Winter in as the starting pitcher. He was hit hard in the first two innings and began the third by giving up hits to the first three batters, allowing a run. That was enough for Collins, who called for Young. Cy Young came in and got the side out without a hit, and continued to shut down the Senators for the rest of the game. Between two games Young had now pitched nine full innings of no-hit ball.

On May 2, the Athletics came to Boston. In a classic showdown between the first- and second-place teams, Rube Waddell continued to prove that he, too, was a star. Pitching against Jesse Tannehill for Boston, Waddell won the game, giving up only one scratch hit in the ninth. (The high east wind, which snapped the flags atop the grandstand straight out, was credited with helping out Boston with the one blemish on Rube's game.) In a fashion that had become typical of him, his antics threw off the competition. After swinging at one of Tannehill's pitches, he entertained the crowd with a somersault.

John L. Sullivan, the "Boston Strong Boy" of another era, was in attendance. He had been invited to toss out the first pitch; umpire Frank Dwyer later said that his throw still showed the strength of the former world heavyweight champ. After the game, as Sullivan congratulated the winning pitcher, Waddell, acting like an excited school child, did a dozen cartwheels.

FOR THE RECORD

The two masters met again on May 5. A midweek crowd of 10,267 showed up at Huntington to see the great showdown. Most in attendance felt that Waddell would come out on top. Instead of an epic pitchers' duel, the fans were treated to a game for the ages. The outcome was never in much doubt as Boston hit Waddell hard all day; the final score was 3–0. What was special about the day was Cy Young alone. Through the eighth inning, twenty-four men came to bat for Philadelphia, and twenty-four men went back to the dugout without reaching first.

As the ninth inning started, the stadium was hushed. No one wanted to breathe too hard, in fear of spoiling Cy's concentration. The first two batters came and went easily, leaving only Young's nemesis, Rube Waddell. The crowd wanted a pinch hitter to replace Waddell, so that the

FIGURE 13: Lou Criger (*l*) and Cy Young (*r*) of the Boston Americans (Red Sox); ca. 1905. *Courtesy of Boston Public Library, Print Department; creator, Edmunds E. Bond*

"record would be stronger." Manager Connie Mack instead opted to stay with his original lineup. Later, Young would say he feared Waddell at bat more than any other Athletic. Although he had a poor hitting record, he was just too unpredictable. To the *Boston Post* Young said, "Waddell is eccentric and erratic." Silence again enveloped the ballpark as Waddell watched the first strike go by. He took a weak swing at the second one, and no one said a word. The third pitch was made in absolute silence. Waddell hit it straight up over center field; Young sighed, thinking for an instant that he had lost his gem on the last pitch. When the ball came down easily into the glove of center fielder Chick Stahl, the place erupted. Young said he felt like a colt. Fans rushed the field in jubilation—Captain Collins and his team circled the pitcher at his greatest moment and danced like children. Cy Young had pitched the first perfect game of the modern era!

After the game everyone had a comment (*Boston Post*, May 6, 1904). His catcher, Lou Criger, remarked, "I didn't enjoy the catching. Young's curves were working perfectly. He didn't throw up two balls alike."

Frank Dwyer commented, "I was proud to be the umpire."

Owner John I. Taylor said he was "proud to have such a pitcher on my team."

General Dixwell, who seemed to be at every important occasion in the team's history, declared, "Never heard of such a performance. I have followed the game for many years. It was a new experience for me."

Even Rube Waddell chimed in, stating about Young, "He is the king!"

Later in the locker room Cy Young sat with a smile on his face, clutching the game ball. He averred, "I wouldn't give this up for a hundred dollars."

As a postscript to the great duel, Cy Young kept up his mastery until May 11. In a game against the Tigers he stretched his streak to the seventh inning before finally giving up a hit. He went on to shut out Detroit in a fifteen-inning game.

PERFECT GAMES

There were actually two perfect games pitched before Cy Young's 1904 masterpiece. Both, thrown in 1880, were accomplished under a different set of rules. Major league baseball has always differentiated between the records set before and after the turn of the century.

Between April 25 and May 11, 1904, Cy Young pitched 24⅓ consecutive innings without giving up a hit.

That year Boston again won the American League pennant. They did not get the chance to repeat as World Series champions, however. John McGraw of the pennant-winning National League Giants refused to take part, causing the only lapse in the fall classic until the strike-shortened year of 1994. *The Sporting News* declared Boston the winners by default.

THEIR RED SOCKS LINK THEM WITH THE PAST

As the 1908 season started, the Boston American League team could look back with pride at its accomplishments over its first few years of operation. The team had become a fixture on the sporting and cultural landscape, winning on the field as well as at the box office. However, even though Huntington Avenue was drawing more fans than the South End, the new team still could not boast the deep heritage enjoyed by the older club—so, reaching back into Hub sports history, it forged its own link to the past. On opening day against the Washington Senators, Boston took the field with new uniforms, sporting bright red stockings, just as the original Boston team in 1871 had done. Gone were all previous nicknames, such as Americans, Pilgrims, and Somersets. Forever after, the team would be called the Boston Red Sox.

Later in the year an icon passed from the Red Sox scene. The immortal Cy Young played his last game in a Red Sox uniform. He was honored in a special Cy Young Day at Huntington, where he pitched against an all-star team from the past. The game was interrupted with applause after nearly every batter, and the highlight came when the aging pitcher was presented with a loving cup, as a show of appreciation from the fans for all he had done for the team.

A STYLISH FINALE

Legend has it that the return of Halley's comet every seventy-six years serves as a harbinger of change. In 1910 the ghostly apparition was seen over the Boston skyline—possibly foretelling the end of the Red Sox's first home. During the next season Charles Taylor—publisher of the *Boston Globe*, owner of the Fenway Realty Corporation, and father of the Red Sox's owner—sketched out plans for a new baseball palace for his son's club. On October 7, 1911, the last game was played at the site where so much baseball history had taken place. The old park went out in style with a Boston victory over Washington, 8 to 1. The *Globe* reported, "There were a number of people present at the game who witnessed the

FIGURE 14: Statue of Cy Young on the Northeastern University campus, commemorating his perfect game. *Courtesy of Dianne M. Foulds*

first one played at the Huntington Avenue Grounds and were anxious to see the last one. There were people present who saw Arthur Dixwell turn the first spade of dirt, and were present to see Jimmy Collins and his boys down the Athletics in the opening game" (*Boston Globe*, October 7, 1911).

Huntington was considered one of the best parks in which to watch a game. The seating was comfortable and roomy. The amenities were plentiful and the light was good, but baseball, and the Red Sox in partic-ular, had outgrown such a small facility.

The *Globe* sports writer, penning the park's obituary, stated, "The old stand and bleachers will soon be torn down, and nothing left to show where once the fierce baseball battles were fought, to the music of loyal fans. In saying farewell to the Huntington park it will only mean a welcome to the magnificent home the Americans will occupy next season in the Fenway." To preserve tradition and continuity, sod from the Huntington Avenue infield was transplanted to Fenway Park.

GHOSTS OF THE PAST

Prohibition put McGreevey's Third Base Saloon out of business. He rented his building to the Boston Public Library for expansion of its Roxbury branch. Where once the elite and the common would meet to discuss box scores and standings, a new clientele took over. McGreevey donated his file of artifacts and photographs of the era to the library, and it exists today as the McGreevey Collection.

Evidence of the Boston Red Sox's first home remains. A plaque is firmly bolted to the side of Northeastern's Cabot Physical Education Center, marking the outer perimeter of the old ballpark. At approximately the site of the pitcher's mound, Cy Young, in bronze, stands ready to throw another perfect game. Finally, two streets away from where the ballpark once stood, the city of Boston immortalized the best fan the Red Sox ever had, with a sign proclaiming "McGreevey Way."

Nuf Ced!

3 FENWAY PARK

Fenway Park, Boston, Mass.

OPENED: April 9, 1912

FIELD MEASUREMENTS:

	Original	*Since 1935*
	Left field 324 feet	Left field 310 feet
	Center field 488 feet	Center field 420 feet
	Right field 313 feet	Right field 302 feet

CAPACITY: 33,925

TENANTS:

Boston Red Sox (American League); *baseball, 1912 to present*
Boston Braves (National League); *baseball, 1914 to 1915*
Boston Redskins (National Football League); *football, 1933 to 1936*
Boston Shamrocks (American Football League II); *football, 1936 to 1937*
Boston Bears (American Football League III); *football, 1940*
Boston Yanks (National Football League); *football, 1944 to 1948*
Boston Patriots (American Football League IV); *football, 1963 to 1968*
Boston Beacons (North American Soccer League); *soccer, 1968*

More than any other sports venue in Boston, Fenway Park fits nicely into the historic landscape of the city. Today it is the oldest park in professional baseball, and is also the oldest existing site to have hosted the World Series, having done so in 1912. Beyond merely serving as home to a baseball club it has evolved into a tourist attraction and, for many, a revered historic site. In a city where the American Revolution began, ether was first publicly demonstrated, and the telephone was invented, that is no small feat. The Boston Red Sox, and with them their storied ballpark, have been woven inextricably into the local fabric. Bostonians know their park inside and out, and are familiar with all its quirks. The "Green Monster" and "Pesky's Pole" have special meaning, as do the last manual scoreboard and the Citgo sign that resides nearby. Back Bay Brahmin, South Boston Irish, and students at Harvard, MIT, and Bunker Hill Community College are all equally likely to be spotted on Lansdowne Street sporting a baseball cap with the unmistakable red "B." More so than the Bruins, who have copped the Stanley Cup on five occasions, or the Celtics, who dominated a decade as no sports team has before or since, the Red Sox are Boston's team. To the faithful, Fenway Park is their shrine.

This most famous park in baseball has also been home to other sports, as well. In addition to the Red Sox and to the "Miracle Braves" of 1914, Fenway hosted the Redskins and Yanks of the NFL, and the Shamrocks, Bears, and Boston Patriots of various American Football Leagues; soccer's Boston Beacons also spent a year there. But throughout its history, Fenway Park and baseball have been intertwined.

The little park in the Back Bay opened in 1912 when the Red Sox moved over from the nearby Huntington Avenue Grounds. The team had been steadily improving and were the Boston favorites, easily outdrawing the older National League Boston Braves. To accommodate the ever-increasing crowds, a Cleveland firm, Osborn Engineering, was hired to create architectural diagrams for a proposed field. The new park would be situated on 330,000 square feet of reclaimed mudflats in the Fenway section of Boston's Back Bay. When plans were completed contractor James McLaughlin led the project. The total cost was $650,000.

The new park faced the same direction as the old Huntington Avenue Grounds. In both cases the third-base line pointed due north. The design

(opposite) FIGURE 15: A postcard view of Fenway Park's main entrance; ca. 1925. *Courtesy of Boston Public Library, Print Department; creator, A. Israelson & Co., Roxbury, Mass.*

FIGURE 16: Postcard view of the Fenway Park grandstands, with the team gathered near home plate and preparing to play; ca. 1912–1916. *Courtesy of Boston Public Library, Print Department; creator, Mason Bros. & Co., Boston, Mass.*

allowed for the potential future addition of a second deck. As is true of much of Boston, the park combined the old and new. The grandstand was built of steel and concrete, but the bleachers, as in the past, were made of wood. Season tickets for a box (containing four seats) cost $250. There were ninety-five boxes across the front of the grandstand.

OPENING DAY

Fenway Park opened on time for the new season. The first game, a "soft" opening on April 9, pitted the Red Sox against Harvard; the Sox were victorious by a score of 2–0. "Real" baseball got underway at Fenway on April 20, after two days of delays due to inclement weather, when

NAMING FENWAY PARK

Team and park owner, John I. Taylor, named the stadium Fenway Park. When asked why he chose the name, he replied, "Well, it's in the Fenway, isn't it?" The name could also be considered an early form of corporate "naming rights." Taylor's family held considerable stock in the Fenway Realty Company.

the New York Highlanders visited. Twenty-four thousand fans came to watch—the game was played under sunny skies, but on a wet and lumpy field. Although the home team won 7–6 in an eleven-inning game, the park's debut did not get the front-page publicity that other local venues had enjoyed for their openings. World news stepped in the way. Just before midnight on April 14, the *Titanic* sank on its maiden voyage from Southampton to New York. Understandably, that story continued to grab the headlines in all nine of Boston's dailies, and the grand opening was a subdued affair. The *Boston Globe* noted, "There was no time wasted in childish parades" (April 21, 1912). The pageantry normally associated with such an event was postponed until May 17.

At the formal dedication ceremony in May, Mayor John Fitzgerald, known as "Honey Fitz," threw the ceremonial pitch. Honey Fitz, the grandfather of America's thirty-fifth president, John Fitzgerald Kennedy, was a loyal member of the Royal Rooters.

Many changes have altered Fenway Park, but the basic footprint has remained the same. The left-field wall runs along Lansdowne Street, the railroad tracks, and what is today the Massachusetts Turnpike. Brookline Avenue and Yawkey Way (formerly Jersey Street) bound third base. On the south is Van Ness Street, and on the east are Ipswich Street and a garage.

BOOM TO BUST

The first season at Fenway came to a climax in October as the Red Sox first captured the American League pennant and then went on to win the World Series. This began a string of victories at the new park, as the baseball world centered on the city for the remainder of the decade. The Red Sox took the series again in 1915, 1916, and 1918, but Hub domination came to a crashing close on January 5, 1920, when Red Sox owner Harry Frazee sold Babe Ruth and several other key players to the Yankees. In addition, Frazee mortgaged Fenway Park to Jacob Ruppert, owner of the Yankees. Legend has it that Frazee did so to finance his Broadway production of *No No Nanette*. The actions sent the team into a tailspin that took a quarter century to recover from, while the New York team went on to win pennant after pennant.

TOM YAWKEY TAKES OVER

As the Roaring Twenties came to a close, Boston baseball was mired in the second division. The Red Sox finished last from 1925 to 1930, and no better than sixth place of eight for the next three years. Attendance

PLAYERS FROM THE GOLDEN DECADE

From 1912 through 1918 the Red Sox dominated baseball with such players as Tris Speaker, Bill Carrigan, Ernie Shore, Dutch Leonard, Duffy Lewis, Waite Hoyt, Carl Mays, and, of course, Babe Ruth. After winning the World Series four times out of seven, the end came crashing down on the team. Financially strapped owner, Harry Frazee, dismantled the club, with most players going to one city—New York. At the start of the 1919 season Ernie Shore, Duffy Lewis, and Dutch Leonard were all dealt to the Yankees; in midseason they were joined there by Carl Mays. The most devastating blow came in January 1920, when Babe Ruth became a Yankee. Finally, in 1921, future hall-of-famer Waite Hoyt joined his old teammates, moving from Fenway to Yankee Stadium. During the next ten years New York won six pennants, while the once mighty Red Sox finished in the cellar eight times.

FIGURE 17: Red Sox pitcher Babe Ruth inside Fenway Park; 1915. *Courtesy of Boston Public Library, Print Department*

RAIDING PHILADELPHIA

In 1934 pitching ace Lefty Grove came to the Red Sox from the Philadelphia Athletics. Grove, who averaged nineteen wins per year, broke the "thirty barrier" in 1931, notching thirty-one victories. He remained in Boston until the end of his career, and is today a member of the Hall of Fame.

Jimmy Foxx, known as "Double X," also came to Boston from the Athletics. Before joining the Red Sox, Foxx hit a career-high fifty-eight home runs. With Boston, he set a team record of fifty in 1938. He earned a lifetime batting average of .349, and is also in the Baseball Hall of Fame.

was dismal. In fact, bleacher damage from a fire in 1926 went unrepaired: the extra capacity was not needed. With new owner Tom Yawkey, though, things were about to change. After taking over the team in 1933, he bought the strongest pitcher in baseball, Lefty Grove. He followed up a few years later, purchasing Jimmy Foxx.

In the off-season before 1934 the young owner virtually rebuilt Fenway Park. Although plans for the overhaul were well underway at the time, a fire in the winter of 1934 made the work a necessity. A January 5 blaze in center field, ignited under suspicious circumstances, destroyed the bleachers and damaged surrounding buildings. Despite the setback, owner Tom Yawkey made his intention to open on schedule very clear.

First, the wooden stands were replaced with concrete. Home plate was moved toward the center of the park, reducing the size of the outfield. Several thousand seats were added in the process. The park was painted green, and left field was reconfigured. The quirky "Duffy's Cliff," a ten-foot embankment, was removed.

DUFFY'S CLIFF

When Fenway Park was first built, and in the days before the Green Monster became the park's eye-catching feature, left field sported a unique characteristic. Up against the twenty-five-foot wall was a ten-foot embankment called "Duffy's Cliff." It was made famous by the dazzling play of left fielder Duffy Lewis, who

had become quite adept at judging fly balls in the area. He would run up the "cliff" as soon as the ball was hit, then determine which way to go to catch the ball. According to *Red Sox Century* by Richard Johnson and Glenn Stout, Lewis once said, "They made a mountain goat out of me."

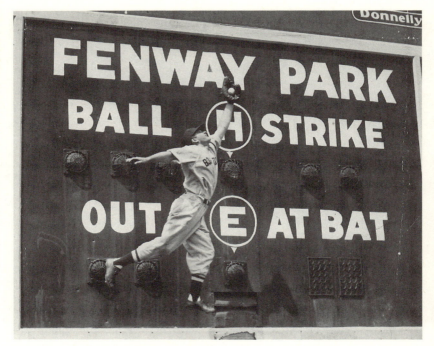

FIGURE 18: Red Sox outfielder Leon Culbertson leaps in front of the scoreboard at Fenway Park in May 1943. *Courtesy of Boston Public Library, Print Department*

The twenty-five-foot wooden wall behind the cliff was replaced with a thirty-seven-foot concrete wall, covered in tin, which was covered in wood and then painted green. This wall, the "Green Monster," pasted with billboards in the early days—is now the single most recognizable feature of any ballpark in the nation. Because Lansdowne Street borders it, limits of left field can be no more than 310 feet. Even this posted distance is suspect. Independent measurements have shown the distance to be 309 feet 4 inches, and even as low as 304 feet. The height of the Green Monster was meant to compensate for the short distance in left field. It also denied a free ballgame to nonpaying onlookers from the roof across the street. Low on the wall is the last remaining manual scoreboard in the league. It still provides box scores of the game and reports on out-of-town action. The astute observer will notice the letters "TAY-JRY" running vertically on the sign, in Morse code. The letters represent the initials of former owners Thomas A. Yawkey and Jean R. Yawkey.

SOCCER IN 1931

In the spring of 1931, the famed Glasgow Celtic Football [Soccer] Club of Scotland visited the United States, touring and playing many of the American Soccer League teams. On May 30 Glasgow was shocked in a game at Fenway Park, featuring the New York Soccer Yankees. New York won the game 4 to 3 on goals by Massachusetts natives Bert Patenaude and Billy Gonsalves. Patenaude of Fall River, who made history at the previous year's World Cup Tourna-ment by notching the first hat trick of that competition, scored first. Billy Gonsalves, also of Fall River, scored the next three goals of the day. Eight thousand fans attended.

Glasgow Celtic played at many other big league baseball parks on that trip, including Yankee Stadium and the Polo Grounds in New York, as well as Ebbets Field in Brooklyn. Celtic went home with an even record—winning three, losing three, and playing to a draw once.

FOOTBALL AT FENWAY

Fenway became an NFL stadium in 1933. George Preston Marshall revived the Bulldogs franchise of 1929, at Braves Field, and named the team after his hosts. At the end of the 1932 season the baseball and foot-ball management were not seeing eye-to-eye on rent so Marshall picked up his team and moved to Fenway Park. (For more information on their days at Braves Field, see chapter 4.) Without changing the team's Native American motif, he honored his new landlords by renaming his club the Redskins. Lud Wray, the first-year coach, was replaced by "Lone Star" Deitz.

The Redskins hovered around mid-standings until 1936, when Ray Flaherty took the helm. Flaherty led the team to a first-place eastern division finish. The top spot guaranteed a place in the Title Game. The league decided, for the sake of fairness, to swap the right to host the Title Game back and forth between divisions. In 1936 it was the East's turn, and Fenway Park was prepared to stage the NFL Championship. As the season reached its close and fans were flocking to Fenway, Mar-shall raised the ticket prices. This proved to be a very unpopular move, and attendance at league games dropped dramatically. Marshall struck back at this impromptu boycott by moving the Title Game to New York. Following Boston's 21–6 defeat at the Polo Grounds, Marshall continued his move south, taking the Redskins to Washington.

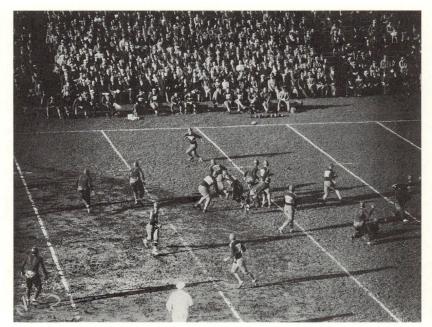

FIGURE 19: Boston Redskins vs. the New York Giants in a 1933 NFL game at Fenway Park. *Courtesy of Boston Public Library, Print Department; creator, Leslie Jones*

The Boston Shamrocks

Boston and Fenway hosted a second football team in 1936. The Boston Shamrocks toiled in the second American Football League. Under the coaching of George Kenneally the team finished with a record of eight wins and three losses, good enough for first place. A one-game play-off was planned between the Shamrocks and the second-place Cleveland Rams, but it was not to happen. At first the game was scheduled for Boston. Because the Rams claimed that they could not afford to come east, the league ordered the game switched to Cleveland. The Boston players, who had not received their full salaries, wanted to be paid before the team incurred the expense of a road trip, and balked at the plan. The owners of the Shamrocks sympathized and refused to go. Initially league officials declared Cleveland the champions by default; later they reconsidered and awarded Boston the crown. The win, as compromised as it was, would be Boston's only football championship until the 2001 Super Bowl (held in early 2002).

An odd twist of fate occurred many years after the 1936 season and the championship game that never was. The Cleveland Rams left the AFL, opting instead to join the NFL, and later moved to Los Angeles, and finally to St. Louis. In the 2001 Super Bowl the New England Patriots captured the Boston area's first NFL crown by defeating those same Rams.

The American Football League retained major league status for another season, but the Boston entry did not fare well. With the core of its team from the year before gone, the Shamrocks dropped out of playoff contention, then disappeared altogether.

Three More Football Teams

In 1940 a third American Football League formed. This time the Bears carried the Boston banner; under coach Eddie Casey the team finished fifth of six. The league limped along for another season, but the Bears did not. Soon after, in 1944, in yet another Boston attempt at pro football, the Boston Yanks came into existence. For five unremarkable seasons the team played at Fenway, finished no better than third, and never posted a winning record. Pro football returned to Boston again in 1960. The Boston Patriots of the fourth AFL began playing their games at Nickerson Field, but started a six-year stint at Fenway Park in 1963.

THE "KID" ARRIVES

Tom Yawkey continued his rebuilding of the Red Sox, bringing Ted Williams onto the team in 1939. The "Kid," or the "Splendid Splinter," as he was known, became the single most recognized player in team history. With a lifetime batting average of .344 and a career home-run total of 521, it is no wonder that his name is indelibly linked with the club. In 1941, he batted an astounding .406. Shortly after his death in 2002, the private club above the grandstands at Fenway Park was renamed the "406 Club," in honor of his surpassing the .400 plateau.

In 1940 the bullpens were moved to right field, bringing the right-field fence in by twenty-three feet, which helped Williams with his home-run hitting. That area of the park today is still called "Williamsburg." Williams did not really need much help in that category, however, as evidenced by his drive on June 9, 1946. His home-run ball traveled 502 feet, hitting Joseph A. Boucher sitting in section 42, row 37, seat 21, breaking his straw hat. The seat is painted red in honor of the feat.

Night baseball came to Fenway in 1947, when the Red Sox became the fourteenth of sixteen major league teams to give in to the inevitable. A set of lights had been used for a couple of football games on an experimental basis, but this change did not come easy for die-hard baseball people. Shortstop and later American League president Joe Cronin said, "Night baseball is a joke, a fad, and nothing else."

TED WILLIAMS

Like no other player before or after him, Ted Williams dominated the Red Sox. Starting with his Rookie of the Year award through his two Triple Crowns, his feats in a Boston uniform have not been equaled. With a lifetime batting average of .344, he retired with the fourth highest record in baseball history. His home run total of 521 puts him among the elite in that category as well. Early in his career Ted Williams traditionally tipped his cap after hitting a home run. He stopped this practice, reportedly after comments were made by a reporter. On September 28, 1960, Williams, in his last major league at-bat, hit one more over the wall. As he rounded third and headed for home, the expectant crowd waited to see if he would once again return to his original habit. He did not. Despite a sometimes rocky relationship with the press, he is likely the most revered player ever to make Fenway Park his home. In 1966 he was elected to the Baseball Hall of Fame, but the true final tribute to the living legend came during the 1999 All-Star game, staged in Boston. His appearance that night, surrounded by all of the modern-day stars, was one of the most moving moments ever to take place at the old ballpark.

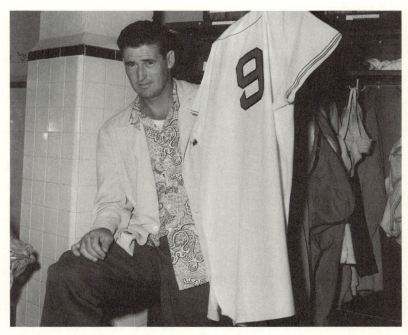

FIGURE 20: Ted Williams in the Fenway Park locker room, with his number 9 shirt; ca. 1940s. *Courtesy of Boston Public Library, Print Department; creator, Leslie Jones*

FIGURE 21: Boston Beacons vs. the Baltimore Bays in an NASL soccer game at Fenway Park, September 1968. *Courtesy of Boston Public Library, Print Department; creator, Frank Kelly*

BOSTON BEACONS

In 1967 professional soccer arrived at Fenway Park. In that year the National Professional Soccer League staged exhibition games at Fenway Park in anticipation of a franchise to be established the following year. In 1968 the Boston Beacons began in what had become the North American Soccer League, and completed a full schedule at the venerable baseball park. The Beacons were introduced with much fanfare. The logo depicted an image of Boston Light, a harbor fixture since 1716. Despite the fact that the games were played at Fenway, the team's fan turnout was only average, spiking up to eighteen thousand when the famous Santos Club of Brazil, featuring Pele, came to town. By the end of the year, all but five teams had dropped out of the new league, and the Beacons had been among the first to throw in the towel.

THE IMPOSSIBLE DREAM

The year 1967 also ushered in a modern golden era for the Red Sox. The team, emulating its old crosstown rivals, played like the 1914 "Miracle Braves" as it left its normal spot, near the league cellar, and became a true pennant contender. The "impossible dream" year had

57

many highlights and a few lowlights, but never a dull moment. The perennial doormats had offered no promise for the season except to "win more than we lose," as new manager Dick Williams announced when the season started.

The magic began early in the year. On April 14, rookie pitcher Billy Rohr in his first start went into the ninth with two outs before giving up his first hit. (Ironically, Elston Howard, who ruined the bid, ended the season with the Sox.) Then tragedy struck just a few days later as young star Tony Conigliaro was hit in the side of the head by a pitch, nearly ending his brilliant career. Conigliaro had hit more home runs by the age of twenty than any major leaguer before him. In fact, when Conigliaro reached the hundred mark, Babe Ruth at the same age had not yet hit any homers.

Throughout the year, Boston successfully battled with Detroit, Chicago, and Minnesota in the longest, closest pennant race in history. There were never more than a few games separating the four. It seemed that when one team won, they all won. When one lost, they all lost. The great race lasted until the final pitch of the season. Chicago only fell by the wayside on the last weekend. The Red Sox had to beat Minnesota in both of the final two games, just to stay in contention. The Sox then had to wait for the results from the West Coast to see if they had fared better than Detroit, to claim the league title. When word came back from Anaheim that Detroit had indeed lost to the Angels, the city of Boston

---

THE CURSE

Loyal fans who have always dreamed of "next year" feel that they have lived under what sportswriter Dan Shaughnessy described as the "Curse of the Bambino." After Babe Ruth, the "Bambino," was sold to the Yankees, the Red Sox—although perennial contenders since the mid-1960s—were not able to win another World Series through the end of the twentieth century and into the twenty-first, while New York won year after year. For many years the four retired numbers of past stars hung over right field, honoring Ted Williams, Joe Cronin, Bobby Doerr, and Carl Yastrzemski. The order of the numbers, 9-4-1-8, eerily reminded those in the stands of September 4, 1918—the day before the last successful Red Sox World Series started. The numbers, with the addition of number 27 for Carlton Fisk and number 42 for Jackie Robinson (retired at all the major league ballparks), have since been placed in numerical order.

YAZ

The 1967 season was filled with unlikely heroes as the team made its rapid rise from the previous year's ninth-place finish. Leading the charge, however, was a bona fide star. Carl Yastrzemski deservedly took all honors that year: he won the triple crown, taking the batting title with a .326 average; knocked out 44 home runs; and had a total of 121 RBIs. His efforts earned him the Most Valuable Player award. He also became somewhat of a folk hero. "Big Yaz" bread was sold in grocery stores, and a song by Boston radio personality Jess Cain immortalized his accomplishments. His tribute, "Carl Yastrzemski—The Man We Call Yaz" was a feature of a radio, television, and recording program called "The Impossible Dream."

The next year Yastrzemski added to his own legend by winning the batting title with an all-time low of .301. What made this feat dramatic was the fact that he was the only player in the American League that year to break the .300 barrier.

He played his entire career with the Red Sox, appearing in 3,308 games—more than anyone had done previously—and was elected to the Baseball Hall of Fame in 1989.

---

erupted in baseball euphoria. Due to the Red Sox's role as the "Cinderella" team of the league, interest in the the team ran high nationwide. Even Ed Sullivan talked about the Sox on his Sunday night television program from New York, and opened the show to wild applause with the announcement that Boston had won the pennant.

The World Series was nearly an anticlimax after the wild pennant race. Most fans, although perennially hopeful, knew that the Cardinals were tough to beat. The highlight, as far as Red Sox fans were concerned, came in game two. Jim Lonborg, ace pitcher for Boston, took a no-hitter into the eighth inning before giving up a double to Cardinal Julian Javier. It proved to be the only St. Louis hit of the afternoon. The Red Sox won the game, but lost the series four games to three. The loss to St. Louis in the World Series did not diminish the amazing run the team had had that year. Between 1966 and 1967 the yearly attendance jumped from 811,000 to 1.7 million. Fenway has consistently registered among the largest audiences in baseball ever since.

LAST OF A BREED

The old park continued to have high points and low in the years winding down to the end of the century. Carlton Fisk's home run in

FIGURE 22: Red Sox 1986 American League pennant, with famous Citgo sign in the background. *Courtesy of Dianne M. Foulds*

the sixth game of the 1975 World Series caused jubilation throughout New England, eclipsing Bernie Carbo's clutch homer just four innings earlier. The 1978 and 1986 play-off and World Series debacles are still discussed among the "disgusted." The All-Star game in 1999—with the appearance of Ted Williams—was yet another poignant milestone in the career of the old ballyard, as the past and present mingled with ease. Three years later, in July 2002—a month after his death—the team and park bid adieu to the legendary "Kid," as thousands paid homage to "the greatest hitter who ever lived," at a moving all-day tribute.

Fenway Park, like maybe no other sports "cathedral," evokes strong opinions and affections. For many years a bar in Denver was named for the little Boston stadium two thousand miles away. Visitors to Anchorage, Alaska, can stop at the Far From Fenway Fan Club, in the center of town. Its proprietor, who never lived in the Boston area, has memorialized the Green Monster on his back wall. The image of the famous scoreboard forever displays the score at the moment that Fisk banged one off the foul pole.

In the October 22, 1960, edition of the *New Yorker*, John Updike described Fenway as "the lyric little bandbox of a park. Everything is painted green and seems in curiously sharp focus, like the inside of an old-fashioned Easter egg." Baseball went through an age of all-purpose cookie-cutter stadiums only to emerge with a renewed love of the intimacy of the old-time diamonds. Fenway Park survived that age and represents a very real link to a simpler time.

CARLTON FISK WAVES IT FAIR

The 1975 World Series stands as one of the most dramatic championship matchups of all time. After the first five games the Cincinnati Reds were in the lead three games to two; three of the five games had been decided by one run. The stage was set for a classic bout on October 21. It began on a good note for the Red Sox as they took a 3–0 lead on a first-inning home run by Fred Lynn. Cincinnati came back, not only to tie the game but to take a 6–3 lead. In the bottom of the eighth inning pinch hitter Bernie Carbo saved the Red Sox by coming up with a two-out, two-strike clutch homer, once again tying the score. In the ninth, Boston had a chance to take it all, having loaded the bases with no outs. They failed to score, sending the game into extra innings. In the bottom of the twelfth, Carlton Fisk came to bat. October 21 had become October 22. On a count of 0 and 1, he hit the ball into the left-field foul pole and into immortality. The image of "Pudge," as he was called, jumping along the basepath, waving the ball fair, is forever etched into the collective memories of New Englanders.

OPENED: August 18, 1915

CLOSED (AS BRAVES FIELD): September 21, 1952

FIELD MEASUREMENTS:

	Original	*1931*
	Left field 402 feet	Left field 330 feet
	Deep center field 550 feet	Deep center field 402 feet
	Right field 375 feet	Right field 280 feet

CAPACITY: 46,000

TENANTS: *Braves Field*

Boston Braves (National League); *baseball, 1915–1952*

Boston Red Sox (American League); *baseball World Series, 1915, 1916*

Boston Bull Dogs (American Football League I); *football, 1926*

Boston Bulldogs (National Football League); *football, 1929*
Boston Braves (National Football League); *football, 1931*

Boston University (Nickerson) Field
Boston Patriots (American Football League II); *football, 1960–1962*
Boston Astros (American Soccer League II); *soccer, 1970–1975*
Boston Minutemen (North American Soccer League); *soccer, 1975–1976*
New England Tea Men (North American Soccer League); *soccer, 1979*
Boston Breakers (United States Football League); *football, 1983*
Boston Bolts (American Professional Soccer League); *soccer, 1988–1990*
Boston Breakers (Women's United Soccer Association); *soccer, 2001–2003*

(opposite) FIGURE 23: Aerial view of a crowded Braves Field in 1933. Railroad tracks run along the bottom edge and Commonwealth Avenue cuts diagonally across the top. *Courtesy of Boston Public Library, Print Department; creator, Leslie Jones*

Braves Field is, surprisingly, the most recently built major league baseball stadium in Boston. Constructed two years after Fenway Park, it stood as the home of National League baseball in Boston for nearly forty years. To help its owners with upkeep, the field was leased to other sports enterprises: Two football teams called the Bulldogs made it their home, as well as a football version of the Boston Braves. In later years the park was reconfigured as Boston University's Nickerson Field and helped give birth to the Patriots. Also playing there have been both football and soccer teams called the Breakers, and additional soccer teams, calling themselves the Astros, Minutemen, Tea Men, and Bolts. The park, however, was built primarily for baseball and, specifically, the Braves.

The Boston Braves were Boston's original baseball team. Starting as the Red Stockings, and playing at the South End Grounds, they became legendary, taking four of five National Association pennants, and then continuing their winning ways through the earliest days of the National League. (For more information on the team's beginnings, see chapter 1.) Their name changed often, finally settling on "Braves" because their owner in the early part of the twentieth century, James Gaffney, belonged to the Tamany Hall political organization, whose members were known as "Braves."

The Braves had fallen on hard times by 1901, and had become the "second" team in town, with the Red Sox in ascendancy. From 1909 to 1912 the Braves were mired in last place, while their crosstown rivals were winning pennants and world championships. In 1913 the team improved slightly, finishing in fifth place. In 1914, however, the team shot out of nowhere, winning not only the National League pennant, but also taking the World Series in four games.

During the miracle run it became obvious to the league as well as the owners that the team's original home, the old South End Grounds, was woefully inadequate for a modern major league team. Through the end of the incredible 1914 season and well into the next the Braves temporarily moved into Fenway Park. This gave them time to plan and build what was to become the world's largest "baseball plant," as the *Boston Globe* called it. James Gaffney parlayed his World Series winnings into a new park. He bought the Allston Golf Links on Commonwealth Avenue, marked off what was needed for baseball, and sold off the rest for building lots. With his real-estate gains, he fully financed the construction of the baseball park at the site. For seven hundred dollars he built a scale model of the proposed park, and in late February 1915 he put it on display. He wanted the fans to know what was coming.

Braves Field, Boston, Mass.

FIGURE 24: A ball game at Braves Field in 1915. *Courtesy of Boston Public Library, Print Department; creator, A. Israelson & Co., Roxbury, Mass.*

The Braves finished the 1914 season playing at Fenway Park, and started the next year there, as well. President Lannin of the Red Sox expected the Braves to remain at Fenway for the entire 1915 season. He had a separate locker room and offices built for his National League guests, and erected a special flagpole so the Braves' World Series pennant could be raised. Gaffney had different ideas. Although appreciative of the temporary home, he announced to the baseball world that his team would move into new quarters by the time they played the St. Louis Cardinals on August 18.

Work began on March 10, but was slow going at the start. Although the site was in chaos for months, by June it began to look like Gaffney's prediction would come true: the place began to resemble a baseball field. It sat two hundred feet behind Commonwealth Avenue, between Gaffney and Babcock Streets, completely surrounded by a concrete wall. A fence sat on top of that. Up to thirty-five feet of land had to be filled in the outfield. Construction of a retaining wall behind center field was necessary.

The stands were the largest ever built, to that point. The groundskeeper, Tom Pallis, who had held the same position at the South End, predicted that every seat would have a great view. In one of the final touches for the new park, he arranged to bring sod from the old home to the new infield. The team offices were at the eastern end of the park. By the middle of July there was no longer any question that the park would be ready on time. In fact it was completed ahead of schedule, but Gaffney stuck to his original date. He wanted to use the extra time to make sure everything was perfect for the opening.

A CROWD OF CROWDS

On Wednesday, August 18, the structure, billed by the *Boston Globe* as the "finest baseball park in the world," opened its gates at 1:30 P.M. Mayor James Michael Curley was the host of ten thousand school children, who filled a large section of the left-field bleachers. In addition to Curley, mayors from most of the cities of the commonwealth were invited guests and sat together in the front row. (Represented were Newton, Revere, Newburyport, Quincy, Salem, Lawrence, Woburn, Lynn, Beverly, Everett, Medford, Malden, Cambridge, Boston, Brockton, Taunton, Springfield, and New Bedford.) The *Boston Globe* optimistically declared, "There is not another like it [Braves Field] anywhere and the probability is that it will stand preeminent for the next twenty-five years" (*Boston Globe*, August 19, 1915).

FIGURE 25: Crowd on Gaffney Street, outside Braves Field. Team offices and grandstand are visible in the background; 1937. *Courtesy of Boston Public Library, Print Department; creator, Leslie Jones*

GEORGE STALLINGS

"Gentleman George" Stallings had a short playing career, beginning with the Brooklyn Bridegrooms in 1890. After one season he left the playing field until 1897, when he joined up with the Phillies for two years, and managed them at the same time. Following management positions in Detroit and New York, he came to Boston and took the reins of the lowly Boston Braves. In his second season he took the team to the top, winning the National League pennant and then the World Series. Although he remained in Boston through 1920, he never again enjoyed the success he had had with his Miracle Braves of 1914. In fact, his team had a winning record only twice more during his tenure.

As fans filed in, the left-field section filled first. Three hundred and fifty members of the Dorchester Catholic League took over the small section in center field known as the "jury box": looking straight on, the patrons there resembled a group of twelve peers sitting in legal judgment. Finally right field was filled. The famed booster club, the Royal Rooters, attended in full force, as they had for every major baseball event the city had ever witnessed. Complete with musical accompaniment, they occupied a place of honor immediately behind the Boston bench. With the Rooters' band and the Ninth Regiment Band, merged during the pennant-raising ceremonies, music mingled in the air with the fans' and team's excitement. After four months as tenants at Fenway the champions were able to fly the National League and World Series flags over their own home.

After the two teams were escorted onto the field the ceremonial first pitch was thrown by Clark Griffith of the American League's Washington Senators. Catching was the "miracle man," George Stallings, manager of the Braves who had led them to the unexpected pennant win the year before.

At game time, attendance stood at forty-six thousand, with another six thousand turned away. At the time it was the largest number ever to watch a baseball game. The *Globe* called it "[a] crowd of crowds for a park of parks," and went on: "It stands as a thrilling tribute to the popularity of the game, and to the loyalty of Boston and New England" (*Boston Globe*, August 19, 1915). The sea of exuberant fans on hand to witness this piece of history, as much as the game, resembled the crowd

FIGURE 26: Lolly Hopkins (with megaphone) was the founding member of a group of female Boston Braves fans called the LollyPops; circa 1940. *Courtesy of Boston Public Library, Print Department; creator, Leslie Jones*

of fourteen years earlier when the Huntington Avenue Grounds had premiered. The main difference seemed to be that the derbies of the turn of the century had been replaced by "skimmers."

A RECIPROCAL FAVOR

As the season drew to a close, the Braves fell off the pace somewhat and their hopes for repeating as champions grew slim. The Red Sox, however, were steaming toward their own pennant. President Lannin of the Red Sox received a telegram on September 22 from President Gaffney of the Braves, offering him the use of Braves Field in the event the Sox made it into the World Series. Three days later, when the Braves were mathematically eliminated from contention, the Red Sox officially accepted the offer. The gift of the field was a gesture of thanks from the Braves, who had moved into Fenway the year before. The Red Sox had a park of their own, which was only three years old, but Braves Field held 25 percent more people. For the World Series there would be no problem selling the larger place out. To get ready for the series and to get used to the field the Red Sox played the last two games of the season, a double-header with the Athletics, at Braves Field. In the 1915 World Series the Red Sox played their "home" games away from home—at Braves Field—and beat the Philadelphia Phillies, four games to one.

FOOTBALL'S FIRST FORAY

In the 1920s new sports joined the professional ranks—baseball no longer was the only show in town. The new National Football League was placing teams in many ballparks around the country. Although Boston was not part of the first wave, the management at Braves Field experimented with the sport, hoping to add a revenue stream by filling more dates at the stadium. On Wednesday, December 9, 1925, the famed Chicago Bears, starring a well-known collegiate athlete from the University of Illinois, Red Grange, came to the stadium; their foes that day were the nearby Providence Steamrollers. This game was meant as a test by the NFL to gauge interest in Boston. The nominal "home team" Steamrollers entered the park first, arriving five minutes late, and were followed by the Bears. There was little cheering for either team. Baseball was still king, and football fans in the area were much more likely to follow the college games. There was no significant amount of half-time atmosphere as the park was cold and the people impatient.

Although a decent crowd of eighteen thousand came out for the game, most seemed disappointed, particularly in Grange, who stayed away from most of the plays—still receiving fourteen thousand dollars for his day's work. George Perkins, a fan at the game, said, "It was more than the mayor of Boston makes with his new increase. Grange got no knocks, which is more than can be said of any mayor." According to the *Globe*, "He [Grange] was a straw hat that got in the way of a steamroller." Providence won the game.

The newspaper was critical not only of Grange, but of pro football in general. The writer declared, "The game was meant for college and high school. If yesterday was an indication of the success of pro football, it was a dismal failure. It lacked the effort that is so noticeable in the school or college game."

THE FIRST AMERICAN FOOTBALL LEAGUE

Red Grange was destined to play another role in Boston football a year later. On October 9, 1926, he applied for an NFL franchise for New

York. He already held a lease on Yankee Stadium for his project. Five other cities applied as well, including a contingent from Boston; all were turned down. Immediately Red Grange announced the formation of a new organization, the American Football League. The first of four by that name, it featured Red Grange's New York Yankees. It also included the Hub team that had been turned down by the NFL—the Boston Bull Dogs. The Bull Dogs, led by President Bob McKirdy and manager Herb Treat, played their games at Braves Field. The home opener was played before ten thousand fans, who watched the Bull Dogs lose to Grange's Yankees 13–0.

THE SECOND BULLDOGS CAN'T HANG ON EITHER

The team and league survived only the one season, but Braves Field hosted a second team, with a similar nickname, just three years later. This time the Boston Bulldogs (spelled as one word) joined the NFL. Eddie Morris was president and Dick Rauch, coach. The team was more or less a reconstituted version of the Pottsville Maroons, a team from Pennsylvania's coal country, which had gone dormant the year before. The owner, coach, and several key players were the same. The team opened on Commonwealth Avenue and was not as well received as the team of three years earlier. The Depression had begun to take hold and money was tight. This time only a thousand fans took the trolley ride to Braves Field, where they witnessed the Bulldogs destroy the Dayton Triangles by a score of 41–0. The second Bulldogs fared no better than the first, however, succumbing after a season.

After a lapse of a year, George Preston Marshall revived NFL football in Boston, forming yet another team. Like its predecessors, the team rented Braves Field. Cordiality between lessee and lessor reigned supreme as Marshall named his gridiron crew after his hosts: Boston now had the baseball Braves and the football Braves. The friendship

---

DOG RACING AT BRAVES FIELD

Judge Emil Fuchs, owner of the Braves and Braves Field, looked for an additional income stream from his stadium when professional football moved to Fenway. In November 1934 he petitioned the Massachusetts legislature to allow him to bring dog racing to the park. He was not well received at the State House. Also, the lords of baseball, still reeling from the Black Sox scandal, wanted no part of gambling in one of their parks.

Braves Field—Home of the Boston Braves, Boston, Mass.

FIGURE 27: Postcard showing a night game at Braves Field; ca. 1950. *Courtesy of Boston Public Library, Print Department; creator, Tichnor Bros., Inc., Boston, Mass.*

became strained during the year, however, and Marshall pulled his team out of the stadium and moved over to Fenway Park after just one season, changing the team's name, too.

BRAVES RETURN TO FORM

In 1948 the Boston Braves of baseball's National League made another attempt at winning back the hearts of Bostonians. It was an exciting season as the Braves won the pennant and the Red Sox tied for the American League flag—the closest the city has ever come to having a "subway series." The Sox lost the one-game play-off to Cleveland, who went on to beat the Braves in the World Series. As the 1952 season wound down no one suspected that it was the last in Boston for the only remaining team dating from the very beginning of organized league play. Attendance was dismal for the year as the Braves only drew 281,000 fans, while the Red Sox pulled in well over a million. On September 21, 8,822 people showed up at the baseball park not knowing they were there for the team's swan song.

The following year the team left South Station for Florida and spring training as the Boston Braves. Warren Spahn, ace pitcher for the team, put down roots in Boston by building a restaurant, "Spahn's Diner," on Commonwealth Avenue next door to the stadium. The groundskeepers were preparing the infield for opening day, when the bombshell dropped. For the first time in fifty years a major league baseball team was moving: 71

SPAHN AND SAIN AND PRAY FOR RAIN

In the 1948 run for the pennant, the Boston Braves relied on two star pitchers, Warren Spahn and Johnny Sain. Each had been a twenty-game winner the year before. Although the team had two other credible starters in Bill Voiselle and Vern Bickford, the jingle "Spahn and Sain and pray for rain" became a popular verse throughout the season.

Warren Spahn remains the most winning left-handed pitcher ever, with 363 victories. He notched 20 wins in eight different seasons. Making this a more incredible feat is the fact that he did not win his first game until the age of twenty-five. He stayed with the Braves when they moved to Milwaukee, but finished his career with short stints with the San Francisco Giants and with the New York Mets.

Johnny Sain had twenty-game seasons in 1946, 1947, 1948, and again in 1950. He was a decent hitter as well, earning a lifetime average of .245. He moved on to the Yankees in 1951 and finished with the Kansas City Athletics in 1955. After his playing days were over, he served as pitching coach for the Yankees.

the Boston Braves would be playing the 1953 season at County Stadium as the Milwaukee Braves. In Milwaukee they broke attendance records, drawing 1.8 million their first year and topping 2 million the second. As if a damper had been placed on Boston baseball in general by the team's departure, Red Sox attendance fell.

In 1954 the park was renamed BU Field, as Boston University took possession. A short time later the university gave it the permanent name of Nickerson Field and it again hosted professional sports. A major part of Braves Field was torn down to make room for university dormitories, known as West Campus. The right-field bleachers remained and formed the north stands of BU's soccer, lacrosse, field hockey, and football stadium. The entrance and offices also survived the wrecking ball.

PROFESSIONAL SOCCER AT NICKERSON FIELD

The Boston Astros of the American Soccer League moved from the Boston College stadium to Nickerson Field in 1970 and stayed until 1975. A second soccer team, the Boston Minutemen (representing the North American Soccer League), played there from 1975 through 1976.

In 1978 Lipton Tea purchased a franchise, and had a very successful year in Foxboro (for more information on the Tea Men, see pp. 106–7.) Due to stadium squabbles the team temporarily moved to Nickerson for

FIGURE 28: Debris from the demolished left-field stands of Braves Field is hauled away; 1955. The right-field bleachers remained and became BU's Nickerson Field. *Courtesy of Boston Public Library, Print Department; creator, Leslie Jones*

the 1979 season, and added new bleachers on the south side, complementing the existing stands on the north. The new bleachers, together with the remnants of old Braves Field, provided seating for fifteen thousand.

Another football team called Nickerson Field home in 1983. The Boston Breakers of the U.S. Football League drew good crowds, but then moved on to New Orleans, where there was less competition for the sports dollar.

THE BOSTON PATRIOTS

In 1960, when the fourth American Football League chose the Sullivan family of Boston as its last franchise holder, the Patriots began play at the old National League grounds. The team name was chosen through a fan contest, and sports cartoonist Phil Bissell penned the first logo. It consisted of a colonial era Patriot ready to hike the ball. The team moved over to Fenway Park in 1963. (For more information on the Patriots, see chapters 8 and 9.)

CHAMPIONSHIP GAMES

In the early 1980s there was a major meltdown of both professional soccer organizations in the country. The American League, which traced its history back to 1921 and the days of the Boston Wonder Workers and Bethlehem Steel, passed from existence after more than fifty years in operation. Two years later the once-proud North American League died too. Boasting such world-renowned players as Pele, Eusebio, and Franz Beckenbauer, and at one time drawing crowds numbering above seventy-five thousand, the circuit collapsed under a mountain of expenses.

In their wake the new American Soccer League formed in 1988, concentrating on the Atlantic Coast. Boston's franchise was the Bolts. In its second season the Boston Bolts made it to the final game of the championship, held at Nickerson Field. The home team was defeated by one goal.

In the third year the league champion Maryland Bays challenged the San Francisco Bay Blackhawks, winners of another league, called the Western Alliance, to a "neutral site" U.S. Pro Championship. Boston's Nickerson Field was chosen to act as host. The American League and Western Alliance merged in 1991 and live on today as the A-League, considered the top minor league in the country. Many of its teams are feeders to Major League Soccer (MLS). Having lost too much money, the Bolts, alas, did not return in 1991.

WOMEN'S SOCCER

As the twenty-first century dawned on Boston sports, a new team moved into the old park. (Playing off the success and incredible fan support for the U.S. Women's Soccer Team—winners of the World Cup Tournaments in 1991 and 1999, with an Olympic gold medal sandwiched in between—a new league had recently formed, called the Women's United Soccer Association [WUSA]. After the 1999 U.S. victory, all players had been divided among the eight charter members of the new league.) On May 5, 2001, the Boston Breakers of the WUSA opened their inaugural season at Nickerson Field. As with the first game at the storied "baseball plant" so many years before, the old park was filled to the rafters. The game result was not a victorious one for the home team, as the Breakers lost, 1–0; but more important to the fans was their chance to welcome their new team and new league to Boston.

BOSTON ARENA

THE ARENA, BOSTON, MASS.

OPENED: April 16, 1910

MEASUREMENTS:

1910	1924	1995
242 feet x 90 feet	190 feet x 80 feet	200 feet x 90 feet

CAPACITY: 4,000 to 7,000

TENANTS:

Boston Bruins (National Hockey League); *hockey, 1924 to 1928*

Boston Whirlwinds (American Basketball League I); *basketball, 1925 to 1926*

Boston Tigers (Canadian American Hockey League); *hockey, 1926 to 1929*

Boston Trojans (American Basketball League II); *basketball, 1934 to 1935*

Boston Olympics (Eastern Hockey League); *hockey, 1940 to 1952*

Boston Celtics (Basketball Association of America/National Basketball Association); *basketball, 1946 to 1959*

Boston Braves (American Hockey League); *hockey, 1972 to 1973*

New England Whalers (World Hockey Association); *hockey, 1972 to 1973*

Boston Arena is a survivor. Aside from Harvard Stadium, temporarily used by the Patriots for a season, it is today the oldest professional sports venue in the Hub. It predates even historic Fenway Park by two years; moreover, it stands as the oldest artificial ice arena in the world. It was the birthplace of professional hockey's Bruins, Tigers, Olympics, and Whalers, and basketball's Whirlwinds, Trojans, and Celtics. The tiny warehouselike building tucked away on St. Botolph Street has survived major fires, massive competition, purchase by a firm intent on using it for a factory, and several changes in ownership. It thrives nearly a century later, having outlived its world-famous successor, Boston Garden.

THE EARLY DAYS

Boston Arena was built in an era before there was a National Hockey League or National Basketball Association, and it was already a fixture in town when it became the first home for local entries in each of those organizations. It continues as a very useful sports and entertainment mecca long after those teams have moved on to newer surroundings and, indeed, moved on again.

The Arena was constructed by the Boston Arena Corporation chiefly as a home for amateur teams, professional boxing, and ice-skating. It has also seen plenty of action in the basketball, entertainment, and political arenas. Heavyweight champions Jack Dempsey and Joe Louis have competed there, as have figure-skating champions Sonja Henie, Tenley Albright, Dick Button, and Nancy Kerrigan. Muhammad Ali trained in Santo's Gym, once located at the back of the building, for his rematch with Sonny Liston.

The groundbreaking took place on October 11, 1909, and the Arena was ready to open by April 16 of the following year. With a stated capacity of four thousand, there were few buildings like it at the time. It was bigger than St. Nicholas Arena in New York and the Pittsburgh Arena. The ice surface measured 242 feet by 90 feet. The engine room contained two 200-horsepower engines, a boiler capable of condensing steam to 400 horsepower, and two enormous 1,000-ton refrigerators. Those entering through the magnificent archway on St. Botolph Street were greeted with a dazzling lobby, painted in at least twelve colors. The hallways were lit by gas jets.

(overleaf) FIGURE 29: Boston Arena with its original art deco façade; ca. 1915. *Courtesy of Boston Public Library, Print Department; creator, Tichnor Bros., Inc., Cambridge, Mass.*

FIGURE 30: Interior view of Boston Arena, ca. 1910. The National Dance Marathon Championship is in progress. *Courtesy of Boston Public Library, Print Department*

According to Jack Grinold, director of Sports Information at Northeastern University, the grand opening was attended by three hundred Bostonians who saw "fancy figure skating" by former U.S. champion Irving Brokaw. The Brae Burn team of Newton and the Boston Curling Club conducted a curling demonstration and tournament, and Brae Burn and the Crescents played a hockey game.

In the early days, high-school and college sports were the Arena's staples, as was public skating; the latter was a popular social event in that era. The Arena was often crowded with customers renting skates,

VOICES OF THE TWENTIETH CENTURY

Many of the best-known people of the century addressed the public within the confines of Boston Arena, including Charles Lindbergh, Amelia Earhardt, Billy Graham, Admiral Nimitz, and James Michael Curley. Every U.S. president from William Howard Taft to Richard Milhous Nixon spoke at the Arena.

In 1993, Northeastern University and the sporting world said goodbye in the Arena to a favorite son. When Celtic great and member of Northeastern's class of 1988, Reggie Lewis, passed away, his funeral was held at the building.

doing several turns on the ice, and ending off with hot cocoa. Northeastern University, the eventual owner, started its hockey program at the Arena in 1929.

The building's role in politics began on April 25, 1912, when President William Howard Taft held a rally there. Two days later his former mentor and archrival, Theodore Roosevelt, held his Bull Moose Party campaign event in the same spot. Roosevelt originally had scheduled his gathering for the brand-new Fenway Park, but poor weather forced the event inside.

On December 18, 1918, Boston Arena suffered the first of many setbacks when a devastating fire nearly destroyed the place; two years passed before it was once again usable. The second grand opening took place as an extension of the holiday season in 1921: On January 2 an ice carnival was presided over by Governor Channing Cox and attended by seven thousand eager patrons. As evidence of the Arena's growing importance, the audience for the reopening was more than twenty times as large as the first such fête only eleven years earlier.

PROFESSIONAL HOCKEY

Professional sports made their debut at the Arena in 1924. In the spring of that year the management was approached with the idea of a pro hockey team taking up residence, complementing a proposed NHL team in New York. Initially the idea was rejected, management fearing that pro hockey might intrude upon the school sports teams already using the ice. When New York decided against forming a team, the plan for Boston was renewed. Grocery store magnate C. F. Adams purchased the first American franchise in a league that had previously been based solely in Canada, and this time the Arena management gave a positive answer. Adams chose "Bruins" as the club's nickname, and used a color scheme of brown and yellow—the colors matched the theme of his

---

RECORD BREAKING DAY

Boston Arena set a world record in preparation for the events on the day of its reopening in 1922. The new ice surface was created in only eight hours "from the first drop of water, to a hard surface," according to the *Boston Globe*. The previous record was set in Pittsburgh, where it had taken four days.

chain of food markets. He built his team by gathering players from the never-realized New York "team" as well as from the failing Pacific Coast Association.

Before the season could begin, a change at the Arena was mandated by the league. In order to conform to NHL standards the ice surface was reduced by eighty feet to one-hundred-ninety feet. A financial side benefit to the regulation was that it allowed the addition of a thousand seats.

The Bruins made their debut in an exhibition game against the Saskatoon Sheiks on November 27, 1924, losing at the Arena by a score of 2 to 1. The league opening came on December 1 against the Montreal Maroons, "played before a fairly good-sized crowd," according to the *Globe*. The Maroons got on the board first, but in the second period Wilfred "Smoky" Harris received a pass from Cooper and scored the team's first goal—according to reports, the goal came while a Montreal player was serving a penalty in the box. Cooper scored later in the period and Boston enjoyed its first win.

THE FIRST ATTEMPT AT BASKETBALL

Professional basketball made its first (brief) appearance in Boston in 1925. The Boston Whirlwinds, of the first American Basketball League, were beaten on the road in Buffalo and on November 30 came to the Arena for the home opener. Their stated intention to the Boston press was to make Monday "basketball night at the arena" (*Boston Globe*, November 30, 1925). The first game was attended by twelve hundred potential fans, who watched the team lose to the Rochester Centrals. The squad was not able to live up to its promise, chiefly due to money constraints. By December 21 the games were moved to the Mechanics Building, and in January manager Sam Snyder moved them to the Mount Benedict Knights of Columbus Hall in Somerville, about two miles north of Boston.

In early February the team's status became shrouded in mystery. The league had apparently revoked the franchise, but details were hard to come by. *Boston Globe* sport writer D. J. McGuiness attempted to contact league president Joe Carr for answers. When his telegrams went unanswered he wrote a column titled "Why The Secrecy?" On February 9, the day the article appeared, the team was going through the motions as if it still existed, conducting player transactions and maintaining its schedule. There were also bad signs, however; the club released team captain "Fiddle" Morley. By February 11, the team was no more. With no fanfare or explanation the Whirlwinds went out of business and a team in Canton, Ohio, got the franchise.

Hockey popularity, meanwhile, soared. Back at the Arena a new balcony added two thousand more seats, and the Boston Tigers entered the Canadian-American Hockey League in 1926. They represented the first of three minor league teams that played in the shadows of the Bruins. The Tigers battled such teams as the New Haven Eagles, Quebec Beavers, Springfield Indians, Philadelphia Arrows, and Newark Bulldogs.

COMPETITION AND CONSOLIDATION

Events in New York were destined to alter the future of Boston Arena. In 1925, famed fight promoter "Tex" Rickard built Madison Square Garden and had dreams of creating an arena empire. He envisioned "Madison Square Gardens" in all the great metropolitan areas. He first set his sights on nearby Boston. It was a city with both a boxing and a hockey legacy and only the small Boston Arena to accommodate the sports. Rickard built the next of his "Gardens" on Causeway Street in 1928. Within a year the entrepreneur suffered a burst appendix and died. With him went the dream of his expanded arena chain. (For more information on Boston Garden, see chapter 6.)

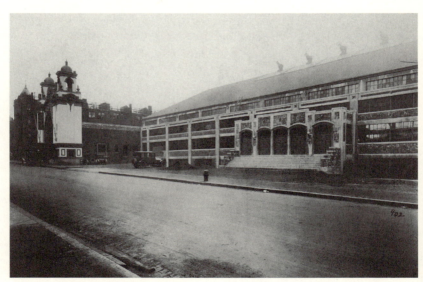

FIGURE 31: The exterior of Boston Arena in the 1920s, from St. Botolph Street.

Courtesy of Boston Public Library, Print Department

THE EDMONTON EXPRESS

Until Bobby Orr joined the team, the most notable Bruin was undoubtedly Eddie Shore. A colorful character, he was the best defenseman of the 1930s and a considerable goal scorer, as well. He played most of his career with Boston, and won the Hart Memorial Trophy four times. He had a reputation for rough play, which earned him more than a thousand penalty minutes. His number 2 was retired and hung from the rafters, and in 1947 he was elected to the Hockey Hall of Fame.

The Bruins, the flagship tenant at the Arena, opted for the new venue and left their original home—setting off a legal battle. On January 7, 1929, the New Boston Arena Corporation, owners of the Arena, sued the Boston Bruins for two hundred thousand dollars and their owner, C. F. Adams, for an additional two hundred thousand dollars. The suit was for breach of contract: according to the plaintiffs, the Bruins had another year left on their lease.

On September 29 a summit was held at the Boston Athletic Association headquarters to resolve issues between the warring hockey palaces. The representatives settled financial issues and made compromises on the location of future events. The minor league Tigers moved all their games to the Garden and the Arena was promised all amateur and club sports, in addition to public skating. Ironically, as the Depression worsened, the Arena with its smaller operation was able to withstand the hard times more easily than the larger plant on Causeway Street. The New York owners, contending with similar problems at Madison Square Garden, made a decision to consolidate and sold off their Boston operation. Although considered a merger, the smaller Arena effectively took over the larger Garden. By July 7, 1934, the two arenas had one management.

BASKETBALL TRIES AGAIN

Later in 1934 pro basketball resurfaced at the Arena. Although the sport was invented in Springfield, Massachusetts, the pro game had not taken hold in Boston, just one hundred miles east. On November 12, 1934, though, a new team was ready to make the attempt. The brand-new Boston Trojans of a new American Basketball League looked much like the Boston Whirlwinds of the previous decade: former Whirlwinds coach Sam Snyder bought the current league champion (the Trenton

BOSTON OLYMPICS HOCKEY

At the 1936 Olympics in Germany, U.S. hockey was represented by a team consisting mostly of players of the Boston Amateur Hockey Club, who won the bronze medal at the Winter Games. Upon its return, the team, already calling itself the "Olympics," developed quite a following while playing at the Arena. In 1940 the "Pics" joined the Eastern Hockey League and won several trophies during their run. Between 1944 and 1946 the Boston Olympics won the league championship three times, battling with the Baltimore Clippers, New York Rovers, Philadelphia Falcons, and Washington Lions.

Moose) and moved the team to the Arena; and "Fiddle" Morley, who had captained the Whirlwinds, was tapped as coach.

Money for the squad came from prominent Boston garage owner Anthony Alving, who had never seen a basketball game in his life, but believed it to be a good investment. Leading the team was Rusty Saunders, an "experienced giant," according to the *Globe*. Three thousand people watched the opening game. The Trojans lost to the New York Jewels in a nail-biter, 21 to 20.

The new team followed the pattern of the Whirlwinds. By February they had moved out of the Arena to the lower-priced Irvington Armory. In a game held on February 4 tragedy struck, putting a further damper on the venture. While warming up for a preliminary game scheduled between the Gulf Refining squad and American Mutual, starting center Leroy Redfield suffered an apparent heart attack and died. The Trojans managed to complete the season, but did not return.

A FUTURE DYNASTY IS BORN

A basketball team with lasting power, and one destined a place in sports history, made its debut at the Arena on November 5, 1946. The Boston Celtics, charter members of the Basketball Association of America, were hoping to open at the newer and larger Boston Garden but a previous booking forced them into the Arena. The Celtics made both sites their homes until 1959, when they moved all games to Causeway Street. The Arena built an eleven-thousand-dollar floor for them, covering the ice surface. (For more on the parquet floor, see pp. 95, 97, 101–2.) The first game was played against the Chicago Stags, featuring the biggest man in the league at 6'9", Chick Halbert.

FIGURE 32: Advertisement for Boston Celtics basketball at Boston Arena, November 6, 1946. *Reprinted with permission of the* Boston Herald

A warm-up game was played, pitting two local Knights of Columbus teams. The main event was scheduled to begin at 8:45, but Celtic Chuck Connors, later made famous by "The Rifleman" t.v. series, shattered the backboard while practicing. An emergency trip to the Garden ensued, to borrow a backboard. Meanwhile, the 4,329 enthusiastic fans were treated to demonstrations of basketball wizardry by members of both teams.

The new team fared fairly well, although large salaries had not yet

THE BOSTON CELTICS' FIRST GAME

Opening at home in Boston Arena, the Celtics lost their first league game to the Chicago Stags in a closely fought battle, by a score of 57 to 55. Chicago forward Max Zaslofsky was the difference between two otherwise well-matched clubs. Scoring thirteen field goals and two foul shots, he accounted for almost half of Chicago's offense. Celtics high scorer that night was Johnny Simmons, who in comparison netted only thirteen points. Boston held the lead for most of the first half and even into the third period, when they could no longer contain Zaslofsky. Celtic Kevin Connors helped keep the Stags' scoring down, but his effort was not enough. With just three minutes remaining the score was knotted at 53. Then Chicago pulled away for good.

arrived for players of the league that later became the NBA. As many as six Celtics lived for a time in the upstairs rooms of the Arena, while trying to earn enough to move out.

THE ARENA IS NEARLY LOST

As Boston Garden grew in stature, it did so at the expense of the older Boston Arena. The larger Garden drew all of the big shows. On December 21, 1952, a preliminary decision was reached to sell the Arena to a New York firm intent on refitting the building as a small industrial plant. In an attempt to save one of Boston's sports jewels, retired naval officer and socialite John W. Watson offered to buy the Arena and give it to the city. Just two days later Governor Christian Herter made his own rescue pitch to the legislature. On June 9, Arena fixtures were to go on sale, but action was delayed pending a potential purchase by the state. Samuel Pinsley, the owner of the New York firm, said he could no longer afford to wait while the legislature made up its mind, and pulled out of the deal. On July 2 the state finally approved the purchase at a price of $280,000, and the building was put under the care of the Metropolitan District Commission (MDC).

During the 1950s and 1960s Arena dates were filled mostly with amateur sports, public skating, and concerts. In 1958 a Jerry Lee Lewis performance ended when violence erupted. Mo-Town groups such as the Supremes and Marvin Gaye also sang there.

The early 1970s marked a new golden era of Boston hockey as Bobby Orr, Phil Esposito, and company dominated the NHL. The team sold out every game at the larger Boston Garden, leaving many hockey fanatics unable to catch live action. To tap into this market the Bruins created a farm team, the Boston Braves, and placed them in the highly regarded American Hockey League. Initially they too played at the Garden and on occasion sold out the house. They set league attendance records that were only broken twenty-five years later.

A SECOND MAJOR LEAGUE HOCKEY TEAM

In 1972, as hockey fever reached its zenith, Boston found itself with a second major league team—with the minor league Braves, the city had three professional clubs to follow. NHL supremacy was being challenged by the brand-new World Hockey Association. The new league saw Boston as a prime site for a franchise as the Bruins could not possibly sell any more tickets, and the minor league Boston Braves were outdrawing many of the teams in the majors. The fledgling league placed the New England Whalers in Boston, and in their first season split their schedule between the Garden and the Arena. The Whalers won the Avco World Trophy and convinced many aficionados of the sport that they were probably capable of competing for the Stanley Cup, if allowed. With the increasing interest in the Whalers, the team switched places with the Braves: the Whalers moved full time to the Garden and the Braves took up residence at the Arena. Playing at the smaller and older rink, and competing with two major league teams, the Braves simply withered away. (For more information on the Boston Braves and New England Whalers, see pp. 93–96.)

UNCERTAINTIES, THEN A NEW FUTURE

In 1975 the Arena was again up for sale. The MDC offered it to the city for $450,000, but the offer was rejected. Two years later Northeastern University stepped in and took over management duties, and then on October 4, 1979, purchased the property. For a short time the name became "Northeastern Arena." At a ceremony on November 14, 1982, it was officially renamed "Matthews Arena," honoring George and Hope Matthews. Mr. Matthews was the chairman emeritus of Northeastern, head of the Matthews Group, and a major benefactor of the Arena. He was also the former owner of the Boston Breakers of the United States Football League. The event's featured speaker was U.S. Senator Paul Tsongas (who later ran for President, and still later was honored in Lowell with the naming of Tsongas Arena); other dignitaries taking part were Governor Edward King and House Speaker Tip O'Neill. As part of the rededication, Northeastern invested $3 million in the plant. By 1995 the old place had its fourth grand opening, complete with a new Olympic-sized ice surface and refurbished lobby.

Like its pro sports contemporaries, the Huntington Avenue and South End Baseball Grounds, the old Boston Arena is now the property of Northeastern University. Unlike the baseball parks, the arena still exists with its purpose intact. There have been changes, however. For instance Santo's boxing gym is now the Varsity Club, complete with theater viewing. Major league teams have come and gone, moving on the Garden and then to the FleetCenter, but the Arena has outlived those eras to do what it was designed to do so long ago. Northeastern's Huskies still call it home, as do the athletes of nearby Wentworth Institute. Local club teams in the Boston City League can still get ice time, and during the frequently scheduled public skating periods, Bostonians to this day lace up and take a few spins around the old barn.

North Station Showing Hotel Manger, Boston, Mass. B-25

OPENED: November 17, 1928

CLOSED: September 26, 1995

CAPACITY: Hockey 14,448
    Basketball 14,890

TENANTS:

Boston Bruins (National Hockey League); *hockey, 1928 to 1995*

Boston Tigers (Canadian American Hockey League); *hockey, 1929 to 1930*

Boston Cubs (Canadian American Hockey League); *hockey, 1930 to 1936*

Boston Olympics (Eastern Hockey League); *hockey, 1940 to 1952*

Boston Celtics (Basketball Association of America/National Basketball
    Association); *basketball, 1946 to 1995*

Boston Braves (American Hockey League); *hockey, 1971 to 1974*

New England Whalers (World Hockey Association); *hockey, 1972 to 1974*

Boston Bolts (National Lacrosse League); *lacrosse, 1975 to 1976*

Boston Blazers (Major Indoor Lacrosse League); *lacrosse, 1992 to 1995*

Boston Garden, the city's second large-scale arena, was built by famed New York fight promoter and owner of Madison Square Garden, "Tex" Rickard.

Constructed above the North Station railroad terminal on Causeway Street, it opened near the end of the Roaring Twenties. It was a fixture of the city's sports life until the mid-1990s, and was home to many sports teams. Playing there were several teams whose beginnings were at the older and smaller Boston Arena, among them the Boston Bruins and the Boston Celtics. (For more information on Boston Arena, see chapter 5.) Additionally, the Garden housed three minor league hockey clubs, the Tigers, the Olympics, and the Braves; the New England Whalers of the World Hockey Association; and two lacrosse teams, the Bolts and the Blazers.

From its inception, Bostonians wrestled with a love-hate relationship with the Garden. In its earliest days it was the three-thousand-pound gorilla from New York pushing aside the older, locally owned Boston Arena. In its later years, it was looked on as a structure long past its prime, bordering on the seedy. The air conditioning did not work, turning basketball games into saunas; During late spring, hockey play-off games were occasionally postponed because too much fog rose from the ice surface. The electrical system was faulty, causing power failures during crucial matches. The ceiling was stained from decades of cigar and cigarette smoke. Opposing teams and loyal fans alike cried foul because of game conditions and antiquated facilities.

Yet still there was something magical about the place where sixteen green banners marked a basketball team's absolute grip on a league and an era. Hockey's most memorable image was born there when a young defenseman flew through the air a split second after his goal won the Stanley Cup. Only at Boston Garden would a general manager have encouraged a legend about "dead spots" on a playing surface.

TEX RICKARD COMES TO TOWN

By the late 1920s the Hub had had a long history of boxing support, dating from the days of "Boston Strong Boy" John L. Sullivan. Hockey also enjoyed healthy fan support, as the city hosted two professional teams and a score of amateur clubs. Serving all of these needs at the time was the relatively small Boston Arena. Rickard had moved on the

(opposite) FIGURE 33: Postcard depicting Boston Garden and Hotel Manger (later Hotel Madison) on the left; 1930s. *Courtesy of Boston Public Library, Print Department; creator, Colorpicture Publication, Boston, Mass.*

FIGURE 34: One of seven roof trusses, supporting the main roof of Boston Garden, is raised into position, July 11, 1928. *Courtesy of Boston Public Library, Print Department*

city with glitz and glamour. On November 14, 1928, lights went on at his four-million-dollar complex, which tied into one of the two train terminuses and eventually included a hotel. In a special ceremony President Calvin Coolidge sent a telegraphed message to turn on the spotlights; this was done using a key made from Yukon gold nuggets. The gold represented Rickard's youthful days in the mining towns. Three nights later featherweight Honeyboy Finnegan battled Andre Routis in a boxing match. Officially it was called Boston's Madison Square Garden, but shortly after the opening the name was abbreviated, eliminating the reference to the New York sports arena.

Rickard acted fast, enticing the Bruins to move from the Arena for the Garden's first season. Although the team lost the opening game to Montreal by a score of 1–0, the Bruins helped Rickard's cause by winning the Stanley Cup that year. Unfortunately Rickard himself did not live to see the win.

MINOR LEAGUE HOCKEY
By 1929 the Boston Tigers of the minor Can-Am, or Canadian-American Hockey League, had also moved to the Garden and held their own in

88

terms of attendance. They were eventually renamed the Cubs, and served as a feeder team to the Bruins. Beginning in 1936, the Boston Olympics, known affectionately as the "Pics," developed a loyal following.

In 1940 the first cracks appeared in the Bruin juggernaut. They had won the cup for the second time the year before, but in January Eddie Shore was traded to the New York Americans for Eddie Wiseman and five thousand dollars. In the 1940–41 season the team was victorious again, but the Second World War began to take its toll, as Weiland, Dumart, and Bauer enlisted in the Canadian Air Force. The Bruins brought up new talent during that era. A sixteen-year-old Bep Guidolin donned a

THE BRUIN'S FIRST GOLDEN ERA

In the second year at their new home, the champion Bruins were nearly unbeatable. In the forty-four-game schedule they won thirty-eight times. Forward Cooney Weiland scored forty-three goals. After that year and all the way through the 1941 season, the Bruins enjoyed their first golden era. Behind the so-called Kraut Line of Weiland, Woody Dumart, and Bobby Bauer, and backed up by superstar Eddie Shore, they were always among the league's elite.

FIGURE 35: Bruins goalie Tiny Thompson stops a shot at Boston Garden in 1938.
Courtesy of Boston Public Library, Print Department; creator, Leslie Jones

HOCKEY ON THE RADIO

1946 marked the team's debut on radio, with play-by-play performed by Leo Egan, well-known local voice. The Kraut Line returned, but because of sensitivities following the recent war, many called them the "Kitchener Kids," after the Canadian town where they all grew up.

Bruins sweater in 1942. He played a role in Boston hockey later in life, serving first as coach of the Boston Braves Hockey Club, and after that for the Bruins.

AN ALL-AROUND ENTERTAINMENT VENUE

From the 1940s through the 1960s the Garden was a venue for all types of important events. Both the Ice Follies and Ice Capades made annual visits during school vacations. With New York and Boston boasting the preeminent arenas in the country they were generally given the optimal dates for such shows, which also included Ringling Brothers and Barnum & Bailey Circus, and rodeos.

FIGURE 36: Temporary wooden track installed at Boston Garden for bicycle races; 1937. *Courtesy of Boston Public Library, Print Department; creator, Leslie Jones*

HISTORY ON ICE

In 1954 Boston Garden was part of ice arena history in a different way. Frank Zamboni of California had developed machines for the automatic resurfacing of ice, chiefly for use at his Ice Land arena. Figure skater Sonja Henie had earlier ordered one of Zamboni's machines for her practice site, but 1954 saw his first orders from major public arenas. The initial ten machines went to Boston Garden, Boston Arena, Worcester Arena, and Providence Arena. That first machine from the Garden is on display at the Hockey Hall of Fame in Toronto.

BRUINS DECLINE, CELTICS DOMINATE

During the 1950s and 1960s the Bruins did not do well on the ice, usually finishing at or near the bottom of the standings. It was at that time, however, that the Celtics emerged and went for a thirteen-year ride at the top. In an unprecedented winning streak, they became the most

---

BILL RUSSELL

Just as the Celtics dominated the league for more than a decade, Bill Russell dominated the Celtics. Although the team was filled with future hall-of-famers, Russell was the only common denominator during the team's thirteen-year run at or near the top.

During his entire basketball career his team rarely lost. In both his junior and senior years at the University of San Francisco, his college team won the NCAA championship. Russell took MVP honors in that tournament in 1955. In 1956 he led the U.S. team to a gold medal at the Olympic Games in Melbourne. He joined the Boston Celtics in the 1956–57 season, at the beginning of an unprecedented run of success. During his thirteen years in the National Basketball Association, Bill Russell's squad won the league championship eleven times; he was named league MVP five times. In 1958 when the Celts lost to St. Louis, Russell missed most of the series due to an injury.

In 1966, when Red Auerbach stepped down as the coach, Russell took over, coaching while playing. He was the first black coach of a major league team since the Depression. In that role, he won two of three championships.

Two months after the 1969 season ended with yet another championship, Russell quietly retired, bringing the curtain down on professional basketball's first dynasty. Following his retirement Bill Russell's number 6 was retired and hoisted to the Garden rafters, and he was elected to the Basketball Hall of Fame.

---

loved and most hated basketball squad on the planet. Behind its new star Bill Russell and famed coach Red Auerbach, the team won its first NBA championship in 1957. The following year, with their injured star on the bench they were only runners-up in the final series, but it would be the last such defeat for years. With (future) hall-of-fame additions Bill Sharman, Bob Cousy, Tommy Heinsohn, Sam Jones, K. C. Jones, and John Havlicek the Boston Celtics won every championship from 1959 through 1966.

As the Celtics aged, it became increasingly difficult for them to win a play-off spot, but once into the championship tournament they seemed unstoppable. In 1967 the Philadelphia 76ers ended the Celtic's consecutive championship streak at eight years. The following season, as they struggled to regain the top spot, the Celtics showed signs of wear. After falling behind three games to one in the semifinals at Philadelphia, a group of 76ers fans marched unimpeded across the floor with a sign reading "Red's Old Men Are Dead," referring to Red Auerbach's older squad. As if that were the push they needed, the Celtics came alive, beating Philadelphia and emerging victorious in the finals against the Lakers, too. The Celtics came back one more time in 1969, taking the top prize at the Los Angeles Coliseum, in what has become known as the "balloon game." The Lakers, sure of victory over their old rivals, had filled the ceiling with balloons, which were to rain down on the new champions; with a Celtics victory, the balloons were never released.

THE BRUIN'S SECOND GOLDEN ERA

As the curtain dropped on the Celtics' first great era, the Bruins' second golden age began. For years the hockey team had been mired in the league cellar, but had drawn well at the box office; night after night the announced attendance was the maximum "13,909," a magic number for Bruins fans for years, before extra seating was added. In the early 1960s the scouts began saying, "Just wait until Bobby Orr arrives." He was worth the wait.

With the addition of Orr, and such household names as Phil Esposito, Derek Sanderson, Gerry Cheevers, Ted Green, Ken Hodge, and Ed Westfall, complementing stars like Johnny Bucyk, the rebuilt team captured the hearts of the city. Social events and town meetings alike were often arranged around weekly "Bruins parties."

On a warm Mother's Day, May 10, 1970, the fourth game of the final series against the St. Louis Blues went into overtime. The Bruins were ahead in the series three games to none, so the outcome was not in much question. Perhaps some thought that nothing could be done to create some drama, but Bobby Orr proved them wrong. Less than a minute into "sudden death," Orr scored a goal for the ages. He is forever captured on film, sailing through the air after he was tripped by Noel Picard—still managing to put the winning goal past Glenn Hall.

AN INSATIABLE APPETITE FOR HOCKEY

From the elite box seats down front to the "gallery gods" in the second balcony, those that had Bruins tickets were the envy of the town. Hockey had become so popular that the Bruins management brought a second team to the Garden to satisfy the demand. The minor league Boston Braves Hockey Club was placed in the American Hockey League and played at the Garden on nights that the Bruins and Celtics were idle or on the road. Management went out of its way to create a big-time atmosphere. A strong team was built, prompting many to feel that the Braves could probably win the NHL Western Division. Although an unpopular sentiment in league circles, many people believed it. The Braves' team pennant hung along side those of NHL teams up in the rafters. On many occasions the Braves games also reached the magic 13,909 attendance number.

BOBBY ORR

Upon his arrival in the National Hockey League in 1966, the young phenomenon changed the way hockey is played. No one, before or since, has dominated as Bobby Orr did. He began stocking his trophy room by winning the Rookie of the Year award. He followed up with eight straight Norris Trophies, for best defenseman. Although Orr played on the back line, he won the league scoring title on two occasions—a first in sports history. The league named him MVP for three straight years, from 1970 to 1972, even as a teammate was breaking the scoring record. And finally, he led the Bruins to two Stanley Cup victories, winning the play-off MVP award both times.

Although his numerous honors tell an impressive story, it was his style of play that stood out. When he was on the ice, all eyes focused on him. He gave the impression that he could play at the game's top level in any position, and maybe even perform credibly as a figure skater as well.

Orr's chronic knee problems cut his career short. He played nine full, glorious seasons with the Bruins, followed by an injury-shortened year. After taking a year off, he spent a short time with the Chicago Blackhawks before hanging up the skates.

WORLD HOCKEY ASSOCIATION

As the 1972–73 season was about to get underway a new major league, the World Hockey Association (WHA), challenged the NHL. The WHA saw a golden opportunity in Boston, where fan support was beginning to outstrip available seating for two teams. Many star players jumped to clubs in the new circuit. The Bruins were hard hit, losing players such as Cheevers, Sanderson, and Green.

Thus, the New England Whalers were born. Beginning with Lynn

GARDEN VARIETY VISITORS

In addition to hockey, ice shows, basketball, and boxing, Boston Garden was the site of many political and popular events of the day. During its sixty-eight years it was visited by well-known political leaders of the twentieth century, including Prime Minister Winston Churchill, President Franklin Delano Roosevelt, and President John F. Kennedy. In 1964 the Garden was included in a cultural explosion as the Beatles came to town.

On September 12, as part of the band's so-called First American Tour, the Beatles came to Boston directly from a performance at the Gator Bowl the day before. The Garden appearance has become part of Boston folklore, as aging baby boomers relate tales to their children of trying to get tickets, attending the concert, or waiting for hours outside the Madison Hotel next door to the Garden for a glimpse of the "Fab Four."

FIGURE 37: Interior view of Boston Garden set up for boxing, with ring and extra seating on the floor. Postcard, ca. 1929. *Courtesy of Boston Public Library, Print Department; creator, Tichnor Bros., Inc., Cambridge, Mass.*

THE BULL GANG

Mike Hartnett of Charlestown worked for twenty-eight years as a member of the Garden's crew, the "Bull Gang." The twenty-five-member crew was responsible for transforming the Garden into whatever was needed for the next event. During his years working with the crew he helped create a beach at the Garden so a touring beach volleyball team could play there. He was there to set up for Northeastern University's annual commencement. The most consistent work, however, dealt with switching between NHL and NBA games.

The ice surface was generally put down once a season, just prior to the Bruins' home opener. The process, which took thirty-six hours, began with the flooding of the floor to a depth of one inch. Once completely frozen, the famous "B" logo, red line, and blue lines were painted directly onto the ice surface. After the paint dried another half inch of water was frozen on top.

To allow for basketball without having to repeat this icing process, two sets of floors were placed over the ice. First came the subfloor. Beginning at the northwest corner the crew placed

252 panels on top of the ice. Once in place the famous parquet floor was laid down "like a jigsaw puzzle," according to Hartnett. In all, the workers linked 264 panels together using 1,056 screws. The crew could transform the Garden from basketball to hockey in as little as fifty-five minutes when necessary.

In a famous incident before a Celtics game, the temperature in the Garden rose to the point where the ice was melting and seeping up onto the basketball court surface. Long-time supervisor Bobby Burke used his years of experience and came to the rescue. He ordered the removal of the parquet to lay down the lacrosse canvas. This provided the insulation needed. With the problem solved, the basketball floor was put back in place.

As the building aged, the Bull Gang was called upon with increased frequency to handle both the usual and unusual. Dealing with a floor cracked under the weight of circus elephants, or shoring up loose time clocks, the Garden crew was always behind the scenes making sure that people like Bill Russell and Bobby Orr remained the chief attractions.

---

native Larry Pleau, the new group built a formidable team. Teddy Green, formerly of the Bruins, was named captain and Jack Kelly from Boston University was brought on as team coach. Many familiar faces from the NHL also signed on. In 1973 the New England Whalers won the first Avco World Trophy, symbolizing the World Hockey Association champion.

Hockey overload finally took its toll. The Braves succumbed to failing attendance after the 1974–75 season, and the Whalers moved on to

Hartford, after a brief stint at the Springfield Civic Center. Eventually that team, along with three other WHA clubs, joined the NHL. They exist today as the Carolina Hurricanes.

INDOOR LACROSSE

Indoor lacrosse, or "box lacrosse," also made attempts to join the Boston sports world. In 1975 the Toronto franchise of the National Lacrosse League moved to the Garden under the banner of the Boston Bolts, lasting one year. In 1988 the New England Blazers of the Major Indoor Lacrosse League played their games at the Worcester Centrum. On September 15, 1991, the team moved east to the Garden and renamed themselves the Boston Blazers. They eventually moved next door to the FleetCenter with the Bruins and Celtics. (For more information on the FleetCenter, see chapter 7.)

REPLACING THE GARDEN

As time passed, many replacement plans were hatched for Boston Garden. One called for a brand-new building in the South Bay area known as the "Palladium." Rockingham Park in New Hampshire was viewed as a possibility. Another idea called for a complete rebuilding at the current site, with modernization paid for through the sale of naming rights. One proposal called for the "Sheraton Garden," named for the

FIGURE 38: Demolition of Boston Garden. The new FleetCenter can be seen to the right, 1998. *Courtesy of Jacqueline and Nicholas Spada Collection*

DEAD SPOTS

Many visiting basketball players charged that the parquet basketball floor at the Garden contained several dead spots, where the ball would not bounce. Rumor said that members of the Celtics knew where the spots were located, and used the information to the team's advantage. Rather than denying the stories, coach and general manager Red Auerbach encouraged the legend.

hotel chain. Finally, when the FleetCenter became a reality, the second house that Tex built went out with style in a week of special events.

Nearly everyone was happy with the Garden's passing but there also existed a nostalgic undercurrent. The place was outdated, with poor seating and no amenities, and had become drab and dirty—still, it was the Boston fans' drab and dirty building. People had grown up with the legends of the parquet floor and its supposed dead spots, and liked the idea that the Bruins played on the only non-standard-sized ice surface in the league. Fans applauded the replacement, yet mourned their old Garden.

During the last week of September 1995, a special show to say farewell to the Garden featured many of the people closely associated with it. Although it would be three more years before the structure was demolished, it was the last event in the building. In the house were boxing greats, members of the Celtics, past and present, and a contingent of Bruins.

On Tuesday, September 26, the Montreal Canadiens came to town for an exhibition swan song. They had been there at the start of the building's history, and seemed to be associated with it almost as closely as the Bruins were. Goalie Patrick Roy specifically asked to play in the game because it was such an important event. After the game, hockey greats from the past were invited onto the Garden floor, introduced by longtime announcer, Fred Cusick. As the lights dimmed and the honored guests exited the rink, living legend Bobby Orr held back just a bit, and took one last spin around the famous, and infamous, ice.

OPENED: September 30, 1995
CAPACITY: Hockey 17,565
    Basketball 18,600
    Maximum 19,600
TENANTS:
Boston Bruins (National Hockey League); *hockey, 1995 to present*
Boston Celtics (National Basketball Association);
    basketball, 1995 to present
Boston Blazers (Major Indoor Lacrosse League); *lacrosse, 1996*

The FleetCenter is not yet old enough to have built a strong legacy. It opened during an era when its two main tenants were not at the top of their games. Despite the newness of the FleetCenter, though, it has a very real link to the beginnings of indoor professional sports in Boston. It is the direct descendant of the famed and fabled Garden, which, in turn, inherited its "big-time aura" from Boston Arena.

The FleetCenter was constructed in the same Causeway Street neighborhood as its predecessor, Boston Garden, and sat just a few feet away from the old Garden (which was later torn down). Filling the same functions as well, the FleetCenter serves as home to the Boston Bruins and Boston Celtics. In 1996 it also hosted a lacrosse team called the Blazers. (For more information on those teams and Boston Garden, see chapter 6.) Following in the political footsteps of the Garden and the Arena, it was chosen to host the 2004 Democratic National Convention.

A NEW GARDEN

When ground was broken for the new arena on April 29, 1993, the building was dubbed the "New Boston Garden." The ceremony came after several fits and starts that had caused plans to be drawn for sites as far away as New Hampshire. The architect who completed the work was Ellerbe Becket, known for work at the Rose Garden in Portland, Oregon, and the Olympic stadiums in Atlanta and Beijing. Delaware North Companies, owners of the Bruins, financed the project completely privately. Fifteen-year naming rights were originally sold for thirty million dollars to the Shawmut Bank; the arena was to be called the "Shawmut Center." Days before opening, that institution was bought by Fleet Bank, requiring a name change to "FleetCenter." In 2004 Fleet Bank was purchased by Bank of America, which will undoubtedly prompt another name change.

The building contains 8,100 tons of steel, stands 162 feet high, 468 feet long, and 300 feet wide. Like its predecessor, the structure houses the North Station train terminal. The Madison Hotel, once attached to the Garden, was imploded several years earlier; the Tip O'Neill Federal Building replaced it. The event was known facetiously as the "Big Blast Down at the Madison."

Ice making at the FleetCenter is done using three 300-ton compressors and more than eleven miles of steel piping. A propane-powered

(opposite) FIGURE 39: Exterior of the FleetCenter, 2004. *Courtesy of Dianne M. Foulds*

NUMBER 77

Ray Bourque is one of the most popular players ever to don the Bruins colors. Playing in Boston from 1979 to 1999 he earned nearly every major award available. In his first season he was chosen as rookie of the year. Five times he was the Norris Trophy recipient, as best defenseman; playing for the Bruins he also scored 395 goals. He retired in eighth place in lifetime scoring in the National Hockey League, and was one of only four members of the NHL to play in four decades. In 1992 he was picked as the King Clancy winner for leadership in the community.

He forever endeared himself to the hockey community on the evening of December 3, 1988. That night the Bruins organization honored former hockey great Phil Esposito, who wore number 7 in Boston. Ray Bourque, who also wore number 7, skated to Esposito during the ceremony, took off his team jersey, and presented it to him. Underneath, Bourque was wearing a uniform sporting number 77, his new number.

The one trophy that eluded Ray Bourque throughout his years in the Hub was the Stanley Cup, but he ended his career helping the Colorado Avalanche take the league title and the cup in 2001. The Denver team that season had a huge Boston following. Not forgetting his hockey roots, Bourque brought the Stanley Cup back to Boston for a special event at City Hall Plaza, where the fans welcomed him home as if he still played for the local team.

Zamboni ice-resurfacing machine replaced the older version, and is considered environmentally friendly.

Upon its debut, the new building housed three private restaurants, open to season ticket holders. The wall at Legends restaurant is adorned with a Boston Garden sign. In addition to the Premium Club and Banners restaurants, forty permanent concession stands and several pushcarts are distributed throughout the building.

BRUINS, CELTICS, AND BLAZERS MOVE IN

Three teams moved over to the FleetCenter from the next-door Garden, two with deep roots in the city and long histories in their respective leagues. The Boston Bruins were the first American franchise in the National Hockey League, and in a slight misnomer are considered one of the "original six" (see box). The Celtics date from the very beginning of the NBA, and are its most storied contingent. The Boston Blazers were also playing in the Garden when it closed. As members of the Major

Indoor Lacrosse League, the Blazers spent one year at the FleetCenter. On November 24, 1997, that team asked for and received a one-year suspension from league play, but never returned.

Most major events once housed at the Garden moved nicely into the FleetCenter. The "New Garden" is the Boston home to the circus, ice shows, and wrestling. The 1998 NCAA Men's Hockey Championship was held there, as were World Wrestling Federation's Wrestlemania, portions of the NCAA Men's Basketball Tourney, the Beanpot Tournament, and the 2000 Olympic Gymnastic Trials.

Representing another link with the past are the sixteen NBA World Championship banners earned by the Celtics, hanging from the rafters at the "Fleet," a reminder to visiting teams of a glorious heritage.

In September 1995, when the Celtics moved to the new surroundings, one additional item came with them, familiar to the team and to all members of the NBA since its beginning: the famous parquet floor moved to its third and final destination. Its unique pattern is associated with the Celtics as closely as the green uniforms have been. Before being shipped to the new building, it was completely refinished. The only change made was to face the Celtic logo in the opposite direction, in order to accommodate the new position of the television cameras.

A popular trivia question among Bostonians concerned the number of bolts used in the parquet floor. The query was immortalized on a popular television situation comedy in an episode featuring two main characters breaking into the Garden to count them. According to Bull Gang crew member Mike Hartnett, the number is 1,056.

Actually, the floor dates to the Boston Arena. (For more information on the Boston Arena, see chapter 5.) Manager Walter Brown commissioned the floor to be built on time for the Celtics' first game against the Chicago Stags, on November 5, 1946. Brown went to the East Boston Lumber Company with the order. Because the nation was still experiencing wartime shortages, no long boards were available. The company

THE ORIGINAL SIX

From 1941 to the major expansion of 1967 the National Hockey League consisted of the Montreal Canadiens, Toronto Maple Leafs, Boston Bruins, New York Rangers, Detroit Red Wings, and Chicago Blackhawks. Although four of the squads do not date to the beginning of the league, the group is known as the "original six."

was able to piece together scraps left over from barracks building projects. For eleven thousand dollars the most famous basketball surface in history was born.

On December 22, 1999, after more than a half century of dribbles, turnovers, fast breaks, and fouls, the timeworn parquet floor was finally retired.

LAST NIGHT AT THE GARDEN—FIRST NIGHT AT THE FLEET

Ceremonies closing the old Boston Garden and opening the new FleetCenter were linked together on successive evenings. On Friday, September 29, 1995, the old building was sent off in style, with vignettes of all of the great events of the past. In a show featuring Dan Rather of CBS News as master of ceremonies, brief boxing matches, ice shows, and circus acts were interspersed with appearances by well-known sports icons. In attendance were Boston Bruins greats Bobby Orr, Phil Esposito, and Terry O'Reilly. Representing the Celtics were Red Auerbach, John Havlicek, Bob Cousy, Jim Luscutoff, and others.

Livingston Taylor ended the evening, singing a special tribute written for the occasion.

Saturday, September 30, the scene shifted next door as the FleetCenter opened a new era in Boston sports. Performing in the new structure was the Boston Pops Orchestra, conducted by its recently appointed director, Keith Lockhart. Nancy Kerrigan, Olympic medal winner from Stoneham, Massachusetts, performed acts from her ice show, and members of Disney on Ice were on hand, as well. The evening was rounded out with music performed by Patti LaBelle and James Taylor.

8

FOXBORO STADIUM

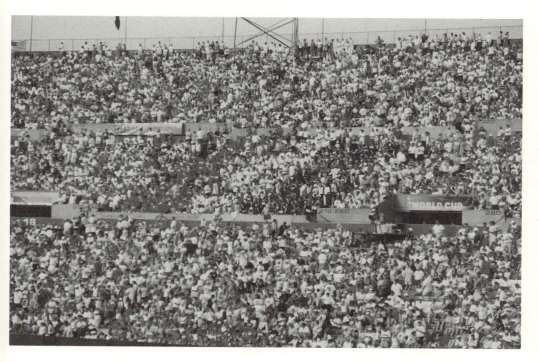

OPENED: August 15, 1971

CLOSED: January 19, 2002

CAPACITY: 60,292

TENANTS:

New England Patriots (National Football League); *football, 1971 to 2001*

Boston Minutemen (North American Soccer League); *soccer, 1976*

New England Tea Men (North American Soccer League); *soccer, 1978, 1980*

New England Revolution (Major League Soccer); *soccer, 1996 to 2001*

Born of Yankee frugality, Foxboro Stadium, located in the town of Foxborough, Massachusetts, southwest of Boston, was a bare-bones structure built at a cost well below the contemporary price for a big-time park. It was cold, uncomfortable, and unloved. Nevertheless it is responsible for saving professional football in Massachusetts.

Schaefer Stadium (its original name) was built as the National Football League annexed the American Football League in its entirety in 1970. The Patriots were among those clubs taken into the NFL. The Boston Patriots had never had their own stadium, having played at BU Field, Fenway Park, and Boston College, and finally having "graduated" from Harvard. It was clear that an NFL team could not survive in New England without a permanent site, designed specifically for the sport. Fans needed a sense of continuity, and the owners needed other revenue streams that come with ownership, such as concessions and rental agreements. Many proposals were made concerning a home for the nomadic club. The proposal for an all-purpose stadium by Boston's South Station came with a price tag well over forty million dollars. The Patriots even experimented with a potential move, when they played a game at Legion Field in Birmingham, Alabama, in 1969.

LAND BECOMES AVAILABLE IN FOXBOROUGH

A break came when E. M. Loew, owner of a parcel of land in Foxborough, which included the Bay State Raceway, made an offer in 1970. He donated the land, in the southwest suburb of Boston, in exchange for parking lot rights. The land formed a natural bowl, making it relatively easy to construct a cheap but serviceable stadium. David Berg designed the field and J. F. White Construction built the stadium. Most seating consisted of aluminum benches. It was often referred to in a derogatory manner as the "largest high-school field in the NFL." The Schaefer Brewing Company paid $150,000 for the right to name it, marking probably the first corporate naming rights deal in pro sports history.

Despite its Spartan infrastructure Schaefer Stadium was a construction miracle. Coming in at only about $200,000 over budget, the overall price tag of $7.1 million was a tiny fraction of the cost estimates made before the plan was developed. Additionally, it was accomplished without one cent of public money. Rather than costing taxpayers, it has actually helped fill the town coffers in Foxborough, through a ticket surcharge system.

(overleaf) FIGURE 40: Women's World Cup soccer crowd at Foxboro Stadium, 1999. *Courtesy of Dianne M. Foulds*

Foxboro Stadium ushered in a new era of sports venues in New England. Such older parks as Fenway, Braves Field, Boston Garden, and even the newer FleetCenter were inner-city facilities. Fans traveled there by streetcar or subway, or simply walked from nearby offices.

Foxboro was built in the suburbs and catered to people driving automobiles. Unlike the older parks, this stadium was not part of a tight community, but rather it sat alone in the middle of a giant parking lot, just minutes from an interstate highway. Scenes such as those in Kenmore Square, near Fenway Park, or on Canal Street, outside of the FleetCenter, were nonexistent at Foxboro, where sports fans did not spend any time at nearby bars and restaurants. Instead, stadiums like Foxboro spawned a new tradition of "tailgating": the parking lot, before and after many a game, was filled with people picnicking from the backs of their cars.

The stadium was never a good place to watch events. Although sight lines were exceptionally good, its position on top of a hill subjected fans, sitting on metal benches, to bone-chilling winds. Plumbing also caused problems from the very beginning. The first game, played on August 15, 1971, pitted the Patriots against the New York Giants. The Giants had a strong Massachusetts following, since for years it had been the closest NFL team to the Boston area—the stands were filled beyond capacity, topping 60,400. Unfortunately, the toilets also overflowed. After that, to its closing day the stadium supplied portable toilets to augment the inadequate permanent facilities.

This incident was but one that caused the venue to become as well-known for its oddities as its sports. The parking situation was also infamous. The lot, unpaved in many spots, turned to mud on many a rainy Sunday afternoon. As the field was built on the side of Route 1, there existed just two ways to leave the park—north or south. Horror stories have been endlessly repeated of hour-long waits just to reach the exit.

Once, during a storm-drenched game in 2000, lightning struck Foxboro Stadium, knocking out the power. And one winter afternoon in 1982, as snow blanketed the field, the Patriots needed a field goal to win the game. The coach called for a snowplow to clear a spot for the kicker. The opposing team complained, but no rule could be found to prevent the action.

In 1982, as the original naming-rights deal concluded, Schaefer Stadium became "Sullivan Stadium," honoring team owner and founder, Billy Sullivan. Through the decade the team and park changed hands on more than one occasion. In 1990 the name changed again—this time to "Foxboro Stadium," a shortened version of the town's name.

SQUISH THE FISH

The 1985 Patriots made an improbable run at the league title. With an eleven-and-five record, they edged out Denver for the final wild-card play-off spot, meaning that the team had to win three road games to make it to the Super Bowl—a feat never before accomplished. In the first post-season match New England beat the New York Jets 26–14. The following week the Patriots were once again victorious, defeating the Raiders by a score of 27–20. The win set up an American Football Conference championship against the Dolphins in Miami. The winner would go on to the big game. History was against the New England: in the previous eighteen games played in Florida, the Patriots had lost all of them. Nevertheless, excitement ran high in Boston, as the team had never before come this close to the Super Bowl. Impromptu support grew as fans old and new began sporting shirts with the slogan "Squish the Fish" emblazoned across the front. Despite the official scientific designation of Miami's namesake as a mammal, the slogan caught on. The Patriots scored first and never looked back, winning the game 31 to 14. The victory broke the "curse" that Miami seemingly had over New England, and sent the Patriots to their first Super Bowl.

The 1996 season neared its close with the first American Football Conference championship ever to take place at Foxboro. (The AFC was essentially the former American Football League, which had joined the National Football League.) The Patriots were charter members of the American Football League, but never before had hosted the big game. New England won the match, but went down to defeat at the hands of Green Bay at the Super Bowl, held in New Orleans.

KNOWN THROUGHOUT THE WORLD

Ironically, though the grounds were built primarily to house an NFL entry, and indeed the Patriots sold every available seat for the final eight seasons at the site, Foxboro Stadium was best known to the rest of the world as a soccer venue. Its earliest contact with the world's most popular sport came in 1976, when the Boston Minutemen experimented with a few games there. It was Lipton Tea, however, which added soccer as a regular attraction. After the Minutemen franchise failed, the tea company moved in. The New England Tea Men, sporting the company's familiar red-and-yellow motif, became a true rival to the highly successful Cosmos of New York. In its first year at Foxboro the new soccer team beat the perennial winners in both meetings. Starring goal sensation Mick Flanagan, the Tea Men drew up to thirty thousand fans per game. However, due to contract and scheduling problems with the nearby race-track the team was forced to move to Nickerson Field in Boston. (For more information on Nickerson Field, see pp. 72–74.) The Tea Men did return to Foxboro in 1980, but never drew the large crowds of the initial season. Lipton moved the team to Jacksonville, Florida, in 1981.

During the 1990s soccer flourished at the park. When the United States hosted the World Cup in 1994, Foxboro was chosen as one of nine venues. As the U.S. team prepared for the tournament, it chose Foxboro as one of its training sites. Success for the team was so common at the stadium that it became a popular site for national games.

Up to the stadium's closing day, the U.S. Men's National soccer team never lost a match at Foxboro Stadium. The Women's National team did

---

MICK FLANAGAN

In 1978 the New England Tea Men enjoyed a brief period in the Boston sports spotlight. Playing to large crowds in Foxboro, they were led by star forward Mike Flanagan (commonly called "Mick"). He scored thirty goals in his twenty-eight games for the team, and was in a season-long race with Giorgio Chignalia for both the scoring title and league record. The highlight of his career in America came in midseason when his team played the champion Cosmos of New York, twice in one week. New England came out on top both times, each game decided on a winning goal by Flanagan.

He came to New England through a unique player-sharing program, arranged between the Tea Men and Charlton Athletic, of the English League. Since they played in different seasons, the teams on both sides of the Atlantic served as player-development squads for each other. Some of the players belonged to New England and some to Charlton. The English team owned Flanagan's contract.

When the press in America took notice of the British phenomenon, so did England. His value went up, making him an asset for the home team. To help fill their coffers, Charlton Athletic sold Flanagan's contract to London-based Crystal Palace, thus ending the sharing of his talents with New England.

In the Tea Men's second season, fan interest waned. Partly due to the team's move to the smaller Nickerson Field, and partly because its star player was not returning, the Tea Men's average attendance took a precipitous drop. Two years later they were gone.

even better. In the five matches played at Foxboro, the women not only never went down to defeat, their opponents never scored against them.

Due in part to fan response shown during the World Cup games in 1994, New England was chosen as one of ten charter members of Major League Soccer (MLS). Robert Kraft and family, owners of football's Patriots, became owner-operators of the New England Revolution. During the initial three years in the nation's first-division professional soccer league, the New England team ranked in the top three in attendance, while placing near or at the bottom in the standings. The 1997 per-game average attendance was 24,423, which led the league. Fan loyalty earned the stadium the right to host the league's inaugural MLS Cup game. Although played between Los Angeles and Washington, D.C., in a monsoonlike rainstorm, the game attracted 34,643 hard-core soccer fans. Those that braved the elements were treated to an exciting game, highlighted by a come-from-behind victory for D.C. United.

Three years later Foxboro Stadium became the first site to host the tournament for a second time. The same two teams battled in front of 44,910 this time. Once again D.C. took the crown.

In 2001 the Women's United Soccer Association finished its first season, and Foxboro was once again tapped for the title game. The field played host to the Founder's Cup game despite the fact that the local Boston Breakers played their home games in downtown Boston, and in fact had not qualified for the play-offs. On August 25, 21,078 came to Foxboro to see two out-of-town squads make history.

ALL'S WELL THAT ENDS WELL

Foxboro Stadium as a sports venue was long on Calvinist austerity but always short on garnering sentiment. It was thirty-one years old at its demise—young for a Boston stadium—but no one lamented. On the other hand, its very existence probably had kept the National Football League in New England—and its last night was something special.

STADIUM OF CHAMPIONSHIPS

When Foxboro Stadium was razed in 2002, it was the only soccer field in the world that had hosted both the men's and women's World Cup games, and had been the site of first-division championship matches for both male and female professional leagues.

THE FINAL GAME

The last game at the old Foxboro Stadium came on the cold, snowy evening of January 19, 2002. In a play-off game against the Raiders, the Patriots had to fight off both the Oakland team and the severe weather. The first period ended with no score, but in the second Oakland got on the board, going up by seven points. After three quarters the Raiders led 13–3.

As the clock wound down in the last period, the outlook was bleak for New England. It appeared as if the stadium would turn its lights off for the final time, following a loss for the home team. New England had performed a comeback, but with thirty-two seconds left the Patriots still trailed by three points. Quarterback Tom Brady had just been tackled on the third down at the Oakland 45-yard line. With no time-outs remaining, field-goal kicker Adam Vinatieri was brought in. At that distance it was a tough play to make in good weather; with heavy snow falling, it was far more difficult. His kick was straight down the middle, and just long enough to tie up the score. Early in the overtime period Vinatieri performed his magic again, scoring the winning field goal. The last event ever held at the stadium ended in tumultuous, nationwide triumph.

Etched forever in the minds of New Englanders is a surreal fairy tale of a game, played in a well-shaken snow globe. Frank Capra could not have written a better ending; it was the year of the Patriots in a year that called for patriots. Having finished the season before with a 5–11 record, in 2001 they climbed to first place, finishing at 11–5. As they had with the 1914 "Miracle Braves" or the "Impossible Dream Red Sox" of 1967, New England fans witnessed a tremendous reversal of fortune. On a wintry Saturday evening with the eyes of the six New England states upon them, the Patriots were on the way to the top of the football world. In its short, thirty-one-year history their wind-blown, ice-encrusted, aluminum and concrete bowl of a home had never looked more inviting.

9

GILLETTE STADIUM

OPENED: Soccer May 11, 2002

Football August 17, 2002

Grand opening (football) September 9, 2002

CAPACITY: 68,000

TENANTS:

New England Patriots (National Football League); *football, 2002 to present*

New England Revolution (Major League Soccer); *soccer, 2002 to present*

The twenty-first century brought with it a new sports palace for New England: Gillette Stadium rose from the parking lot of its predecessor field, Foxboro Stadium. Built by the Kraft family with private funds, it houses their New England Patriots as well as their soccer team, the New England Revolution.

After a decade of nomadic existence, followed by thirty-one years in a barely adequate stadium, the New England Patriots have a place they can proudly call home. Following in the footsteps of the "Miracle Braves" of 1914, the team finished near the bottom the year before in an antiquated park, rose to become the surprise kings of their sport, and celebrated the unexpected win in a brand-new stadium the following year.

A NEW STADIUM IS NEEDED

The utilitarian Schaefer (later Foxboro) Stadium had served its purpose but had never been a satisfying final stop, either in the eyes of team owners or fans. (For more information on Foxboro Stadium, see chapter 8.) Throughout much of their stay, rumor had it that the Patriots were going to go elsewhere.

Elaborate designs were drawn for a stadium in South Boston, but were not approved; Providence, Rhode Island, was also considered. In November 1998 the team nearly packed its bags and moved to Hartford. In that scenario the Patriots were to play in a brand-new sixty-eight-thousand-seat park at Adrian's Landing, as part of a one-billion-dollar development project. Financing was in place—the stadium would be paid for through the sale of bonds and a special tax on tickets. The University of Connecticut football team was to play there, as well. By June 1999 the deal had fallen through, in part because under the schedule, the Patriots would begin play no earlier than 2003, and so attention again turned to the town of Foxborough, host to the team since 1971.

The new, thoroughly modern facility next door to the Pats' former home is filled both with amenities and character. It is named for Boston-based shaving and personal products giant, Gillette, which purchased naming rights. Gillette Stadium was initially to be named for an Andover, Massachusetts, Internet firm, CMGI, which purchased the naming rights for fifteen years. Although soccer games and concerts were held there under the name CMGI Field, it was changed before the Patriots opened their inaugural season, as the owners struck a deal with Gillette.

(opposite) FIGURE 41: Gillette Stadium looking north toward lighthouse and bridge, 2003. *Courtesy of Dianne M. Foulds*

THE NEW STADIUM

The $325-million stadium covers a seventeen-acre plot, more than three times the size of the old structure. It holds sixty-eight thousand seats, of which six thousand are club seats, and eighty-one boxes contain two thousand more seats. There are fifteen souvenir stands and two giant video screens, each forty-eight feet by twenty-seven feet. Two video strips run the length of the side stands, and there are one thousand television monitors and two thousand speakers. The concession stands all have been given names with a New England flair—"Boston Common," "Federal Hill," and "Freeport." Walking through the north gate one is greeted with a miniaturized light house overlooking a replica of the Longfellow Bridge.

Soft Opening

The first event was a "soft opening" featuring the other tenants, the New England Revolution. The "Revs," as the fans have dubbed them, met the Dallas Burn in a Major League Soccer game on an evening marked with perfect weather. As the park was not yet complete, ticket sales for the opening match were limited, but the 22,006 available seats sold out fast.

The evening began with a contented tailgating crowd having dinner in the parking lot. As if a sign of things to come, a rainbow appeared above the remnants of the old stadium at the top of the hill. Team and stadium owner Robert Kraft greeted his guests at the entrance and in the concourse of his fantastic new sports palace. Prior to the opening kickoff, as the national anthem played, small fireworks burst overhead to coincide with the "rockets red glare, and bombs bursting in air."

Exactly five minutes and ten seconds after the referee blew the opening whistle, Taylor Twellman of the home team scored the first goal in Gillette Stadium history. As if the game were scripted, the New England Revolution, which had struggled on the field throughout its entire existence, looked in command at the opener, just as it should on such an occasion. Taylor Twellman scored twice in the first half and the score stood at 2–0 in favor of New England.

At half time, "Beautiful Day," by the band U2, blared through the new speaker system, coinciding with another large fireworks display above and behind the video screen at the south end. The song had become an unofficial anthem for the stadium during weeks of preparation, since the same band had performed at the previous year's Super Bowl. No more goals were recorded in the second half; New England won the game.

FIGURE 42: Tailgaters in the parking lot of Gillette Stadium, awaiting the start of a game. The remnants of the old Foxboro Stadium can be seen at the top of the photo, 2002. *Courtesy of Lillian M. Foulds*

That evening, as the field joined the ranks of Boston ballparks — with such hallowed forerunners as Fenway Park, Braves Field, and the Huntington Avenue and South End Grounds — owner Robert Kraft undoubtedly agreed with the song's title.

First Patriots Game

On August 17, 2002, the New England Patriots inaugurated their brand-new Gillette Stadium with an exhibition-game win over the Philadelphia Eagles. In a closely fought match the home team won by a score of 16–15. Although this was not an official league game, the crowd arrived early and in droves. The parking lot was full four hours before the first kickoff. After several false starts and potential moves in the Patriots' search for a home, the opening of the stadium marked the beginning of a new era for the team. The ever-loyal fans were there to be a part of it. A full house of 68,436 was on hand to watch the first homecoming of the recently crowned Super Bowl champions.

In the first quarter the Patriots got on the board with a twenty-seven-yard field goal by Adam Vinatieri; this was, appropriately, the first score at Gillette Stadium. In the final game at the old park next door, Vinatieri's

FIGURE 43: New England Patriots' 2001 Super Bowl Championship banner at Gillette Stadium. *Courtesy of Dianne M. Foulds*

game-winning field goal had marked the last points scored at that venue. He had also kicked the game-winning points in the 2002 Super Bowl.

Grand Opening

Pomp and circumstance was the order of the day on September 9, 2002. Exactly forty-two years after the Patriots franchise played its first official league game, it opened a brand-new stadium—entering the field as reigning Super Bowl champions.

The ceremonies began precisely at 8:30 P.M. with a moment of silence in remembrance of those lost on September 11, 2001, nearly a year before. Next came the presentation of historical footage (shown on the giant video screens) chronicling the team's former homes. Team owner Robert Kraft then welcomed the crowd to Gillette Stadium, followed immediately by a laser and fireworks display focused on the lighthouse at the entrance.

U2's "Beautiful Day" played while highlights of the previous year's successful play-off and Super Bowl run were shown. Finally came the unveiling of the championship banner, accompanied by "Ode to Joy" from Beethoven's Ninth Symphony and more fireworks. Former president George H. W. Bush, honorary team captain, took part in the ceremonial coin toss, and the game began at 9:12 P.M.

After the team's unlikely Super Bowl victory the year before, head

---

ALMOST ANOTHER CHAMPION

For the third time in seven years the town of Foxborough was chosen to host the Major League Soccer championship game. The first two were held in the old Foxboro Stadium, and the third was at brand-new Gillette Stadium. Although the New England Revolution struggled on the field through the early years, the team had always drawn well. The 2002 season began poorly and the chances that the Revolution would play in the title game, which they were to host, were slim. Under their new coach, Steve Nicol, however, they came to life. They finished the season in first place, and earned a berth in the championship at their own home. Playing the heavily favored Los Angeles Galaxy in front of a packed Gillette Stadium, they nearly won. At the end of regulation time the teams were tied. In the second "golden goal" period, Revolution striker Winston Griffiths banged one off the crossbar and nearly earned the trophy. Heartbreak set in just a minute later as Carlos Ruiz of Los Angeles netted the winner for the visitors.

coach Bill Belichick quipped that if the Patriots played again the following week they would still not be considered the favorites to win. His words proved prophetic. Despite their victory over the same team in the conference championship in January, and their current home-field advantage, the Patriots entered the match as three-point underdogs. The end result, however, was much the same. Within three minutes of the opening kickoff the Pittsburgh squad had committed two turnovers. Four minutes and three seconds into the game the Patriots took the lead as quarterback Tom Brady threw a pass to tight end Christian Fauria, scoring the first official points at Gillette. The New England Patriots completed the night of celebration by winning the game, 30–14.

Followers of Boston sports today may view such local favorites as the Red Sox or Bruins as permanent fixtures. The teams have existed long enough for our grandparents to have been fans, and we assume they will be around for our grandchildren to root for as well. They have earned their aura of permanence through a combination of high-level play, customer support, and longevity.

For each successful franchise there have been many failures. Some of the organizations that did not stand the test of time had spectacular starts, giving the impression that they were in it for the long haul. Some even built their own impressive stadiums.

Dedicated with as much fanfare as places like Fenway Park or Braves Field, there were six stadiums that seemed destined to join the ranks of the local sports shrines, but did not. They were opened with band concerts, visiting dignitaries, and naming contests. They were praised in the newspapers for their sight lines and comfort, and they had spectacular "careers" in the major leagues. Their stay among the elite, however, proved short-lived.

The doomed teams and their homes did not survive for a variety of reasons. Competition from established organizations was brutal to the newcomers. In some cases the leagues collapsed around them. In others, the site was not right, or the public simply wasn't interested.

These forgotten parks, with one exception, have been completely erased from the landscape, and sometimes barely exist even in the

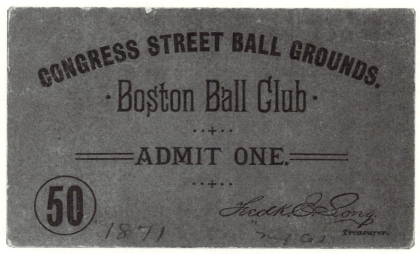

FIGURE 44: Season pass for the Boston Players League team at the Congress Street Grounds; 1890. *Courtesy of Boston Public Library, Print Department*

memories of New England sports fans. Today, citizens shop, study, or work at the sites, with no idea of the games played there, or of the thousands of supporters who once cheered on the participants.

One is still used for its original purpose. The grandstand is long gone, but the playing field still hosts the sport it was built for so long ago. Today, though, no national cup tournaments would be considered for the spot, and no teams from New York, Philadelphia, Baltimore, or other far-off places are likely to visit. Instead the park is filled with hundreds of youth teams, whose members have no idea of the history once played out on what is now their field.

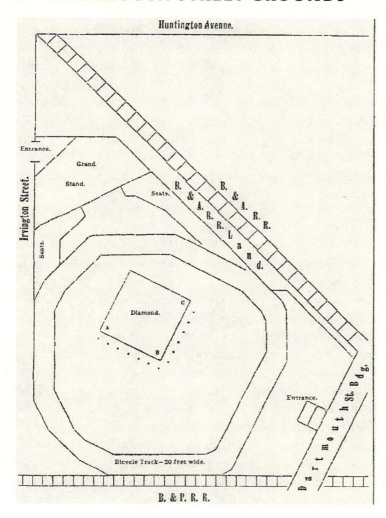

OPENED: April 30, 1884

CLOSED: 1897

FIELD MEASUREMENTS: Left field 315 feet (approximately), Deep center field 420 feet, Right field 315 feet

CAPACITY: 4,649

TENANTS:

Boston Unions (Union Association); *baseball, 1884*

Boston Blues (Eastern Baseball League); *baseball, 1886*

In a triangle that currently houses the Copley Place shopping mall once sat the first challenge to the Boston Braves of the National League. The field, home to the New England entry into the upstart baseball league called the Union Association, was fitted into a piece of Back Bay land bounded on two sides by railroad tracks and on the third by Irvington Street, which no longer exists. The new team had no formal name, but contemporary newspapers referenced them as the "Boston Unions." Ironically, the park was called the Dartmouth Street Grounds, although only a few feet of the park touched that thoroughfare. The complex was built in just six weeks in the spring of 1884, but its owners boasted of a facility far in advance of any of its predecessors. It disappeared from the local sports scene nearly as fast as it came. Today as shoppers frequent the department stores, theaters, and restaurants, few, if any, realize the footnote to Boston sports history that the site owns.

A CHALLENGE TO THE OLD ORDER

The Union Association was the brainchild of sports entrepreneur Henry Lucas, of St. Louis. It was born in late 1883 out of opposition to the so-called reserve clause.

The Union Association (UA) was the first of two leagues formed in opposition to organized baseball's reserve clause, which effectively bound players to one baseball team for life. Movement from one team to another was done only at the pleasure of the owners. The clause came into existence in 1879 as a secret agreement between team owners, reserving five players for each team. The chosen players could not be signed by any other team without the owner's permission. The agreement was later expanded to include all team members.

Developing concurrently with the formation of the UA was a plan by Connecticut native Thomas Furniss to create a new sports association in the Hub. He envisioned the building of a complex to house several sports, including baseball. Since the National League was already firmly entrenched at the South End Grounds with the Braves, he opted for a franchise in the new circuit. Unfortunately he was not able to follow through on his plan, but Henry Lucas was sold on the idea of a Boston entry in his new league. He held a spot open for the city for quite some time, but as the season opening neared he took action himself. On March 3, 1884, he came to town to meet with the baseball movers and shakers

(overleaf) FIGURE 45: Newspaper map of the Dartmouth Street Grounds, in Boston's Back Bay; *Boston Globe*, 1884. *Reprinted courtesy of* The Boston Globe

TIM MURNANE

The first manager for the Boston Unions was infielder Tim Murnane (sometimes spelled "Murnan"). Born in Connecticut, he started his career with the Middletown Mansfields where his .359 batting average was his career high. He moved around among the National Association teams, landing in Boston in 1876, where he played for two years before moving south to Providence. He came out of a five-year retirement to both play for and manage the Union Association team in Boston during the 1884 season.

He returned to the Dartmouth Street Grounds two years later, ending his baseball career as owner of the minor league Boston Blues.

---

of the era. He also visited the former circus grounds off of Dartmouth Street, site of Furniss's proposed park, and declared the spot quite adequate for his purposes. While in Boston, he received a financial commitment from former local sports hero George Wright, who had become a partner in Wright and Ditson, sporting goods. Lucas also put up fifteen hundred dollars of his own money to help assure that a team would be placed in one of the hotbeds of the national pastime, and signed a three-year lease, with a five-year option, for the Dartmouth Street property.

A stock company was organized for the purpose of raising ten thousand dollars to build the team and stadium. That amount was later amended to twenty-five thousand dollars—two hundred fifty shares at one hundred dollars each. According to the *Boston Globe*, Wright made it clear that the time to build a pennant contender in the first year was probably too short, but using mostly local talent the team could create a solid foundation for the 1885 season. Three well-known players, who had all been members of Boston's National League Braves, were signed. Former battery mates Thomas Bond and Lewis "Blower" Brown from Leominster were joined again; they had once plied their trade together at the South End Grounds. First baseman Tim Murnane was named player-manager.

HOUSING THE NEW TEAM

On March 20, with only a month left before the opening pitch, architect S. J. F. Thayer was chosen to draw up plans for the timberwork of the new field. On April 3, all contracts were finalized, and grading work began.

The structure covered 134,000 square feet, facing roughly southeast. The 7,039-square-foot grandstand was on the northwest corner, on

Irvington Street, not far from Huntington Avenue. The diamond faced the Boston and Providence Railroad tracks so the afternoon sun would not impede in the spectators' view of the game. According to both the *Boston Globe* and *Boston Herald*, the grandstand was in the shape of an octagon "cut in half diagonally," of "Moorish" design, and holding 1,589 seats. The façade was 140 feet long with 54-foot sides, and a roof 40 feet above. Directly in front of the building was a gigantic flagpole, which also served as part of the support. The walls were made of corrugated iron, painted in bright colors. Home plate was situated 90 feet from the front of the building, with the entire length of the spacious park being 680 feet. It was thought that no one would ever put a ball out of the park in center field.

In addition to the regular admission seats were luxury boxes, an innovation in sports. On both sides of the grandstand were three of these boxes, each with room for eight to ten people. The boxes had private entrances, and according to the *Globe* they were meant "for those who want to attend ball games but want to be separate from the crowd." Stretching from each side of the grandstand were sets of uncovered seats. Each side of bleachers contained room for fifteen hundred patrons.

Placed under the grandstand were team and corporate offices, locker rooms, rest rooms, a Western Union telegraph office, a concession stand, and a restaurant.

The company had high hopes that the grounds would become a center for sports of all types in Boston. A running and bicycle track ringed the diamond. The five-lap track was twenty feet wide and was constructed with leading-edge technology to assure that it was among the fastest in the nation. It had a ten-inch foundation of broken stone covered by two inches of binding gravel. Topping it off were two inches of hard-packed cinder. The track was at the extreme edge of the park on the left- and right-field sides, hugging the pair of railroad tracks. Future plans included facilities for lawn tennis and lacrosse, and rental commitments had already been received from the amateur Commercial Baseball Association and the Beacons. Bicycle races were scheduled and the Union Amateur Athletic Club and Wells Athletic Club planned to use the site for practice.

There were two entrances to the park. The first was on Dartmouth Street, where patrons descended onto the field using a stairway left from the circus days. The second was on Irvington Street, where those holding tickets to the main structure entered on the second level, directly into the seating area. Surrounding the park was a twelve-foot fence topped with four-foot lattice work, making it difficult for passersby to watch the game without paying. On the two sides abutting the tracks, canvas was stretched between telegraph poles to keep foul balls from hitting passing trains.

The owners felt that the location and accessibility were unsurpassed, with two railroads running by the park and horsecar lines plentiful. One made a stop at the Dartmouth Street entrance, while the Columbus Avenue line came close to the Irvington Street side.

With lightninglike speed the stadium was nearly completed in time for the home opener. The roof had yet to be installed over the grandstand, and although the infield was planted with "the best Somerville sod," according to the *Boston Herald*, the outfield remained as dirt. All but about a hundred seats were in place. By most accounts, however, patrons were subjected to no inconveniences.

PLAY BALL!

Opening day, April 30, was a beautiful spring afternoon, in contrast to the weeks of dismal, damp weather Boston had been experiencing. After a short band concert, the Unions made their first appearance. Their uniforms, manufactured by Wright and Ditson, were said by the *Boston Globe* to be different from any previously seen in Boston. They consisted of "white breeches, dark blue stockings, belt and shirt, and cap of small black and white check" (*Boston Herald*, April 5, 1884).

Baseball fans had eagerly anticipated the first game at Dartmouth Street. Despite warnings that the team would not be a powerhouse in its inaugural season, it had just returned from a highly successful road trip. In the first three games at Philadelphia against the Keystones, Boston had swept the series; in Washington, against the Nationals, they had taken two of three and become the talk of the baseball world. More than twenty-eight hundred spectators arrived to see the return match against Philadelphia. Although Boston easily won the opener by a score of 15 to 8, most sportswriters commented that play by both teams was sloppy, and not up to the standard of the National League.

The team came back to earth somewhat and settled into the middle of the standings, finishing with a respectable but unremarkable 58–51 record. It was good enough for fifth place out of thirteen. The Unions changed personnel frequently during the season, hiring new managers twice. Thomas Furniss, who had originally attempted to become the owner of the Boston franchise, even had a short stint in the job. Although Boston supported the new team at the gate, the league drowned in a

125

sea of red ink. Henry Lucas abandoned the sinking ship and obtained a National League franchise for himself. After only one season the new team and its league were no more.

The park lived on for a while, though. In 1886 the team even came back to life, in a way. The original manager, Tim Murnane, obtained a minor league franchise in the Eastern Baseball League; he called his team the Boston Blues and served as team manager. He arranged with his former employer, the Union Athletic Association, to rent the Dartmouth Street Grounds. Under a verbal contract, according to Murnane, the park owner would receive 50 percent of the net profits.

NO ADMISSION

On April 22, 1886, Murnane's Boston Blues entered the park with appropriate blue uniforms and white stockings, to the applause of the 450 attendees. For the next few days the team continued to draw similar crowds, but a showdown on April 29 altered the future of both team and stadium.

When baseball fans arrived at the park, they were met by two policemen blocking the entrance to the bridge from Huntington Avenue. There was no word of explanation, so rumors abounded. Some thought the team had gone on strike. As the mystery grew, the crowd increased. A representative of the field owner arrived but refused to offer an explanation. He instructed the police to keep up their guard. At about 3 P.M. the team arrived and also could not gain admittance. Meanwhile, Blues Manager Murnane attempted to negotiate with Frank Winslow, president of the Union Athletic Association. Apparently Winslow now insisted that the rent was equal to half the receipts, rather than profits, and that he required a deposit of three hundred dollars to open the gates. Arthur Soden, president of the Braves, arrived by hack. He had received word of the impasse and came armed with a permit for the Blues to play at his South End Grounds. Following a mighty cheer for the baseball savior, the crowd filled up all available horsecars, while many left on foot for the National League park in the South End.

Later in the day Murnane struck a deal with Soden to play the remainder of the Eastern League schedule at the South End on days that the Braves were on the road, thus ending baseball at Dartmouth Street.

PLAYING A PART IN STARTING A TRADITION

Before the end of the decade a portion of the field was taken for the construction of the Irvington Street Armory, where the Massachusetts

National Guard conducted drills. The remainder of the field, renamed the Irvington Oval, was used for a few years to host track meets sponsored by the Boston Athletic Association (BAA). In 1897 the field saw one last glimpse of glory, serving as the original finish line of the Boston Marathon. On April 19, 1897, in a celebration of Patriot's Day in Massachusetts the BAA held a series of events on the field during the morning, with the grand finale being the finish of the marathon. Starting twenty-six miles away in Ashland at noon, the frontrunners approached the former Dartmouth Street Grounds shortly before 3 P.M. "Five hundred had assembled [at the BAA clubhouse] to cheer the victor," wrote the *Boston Globe.*

The crowd, shouting "Bravo!" formed a pathway as the leader, J. J. McDermott, crossed Huntington Avenue, turned onto Irvington, and finally into the oval. According to the *Globe* the cheers were deafening. To finish the race, the runners were required to make one lap around the track. McDermott had some trouble negotiating the track as it was filled with well-wishers, all wanting to shake the hand of the first victor. When it was announced that his time of two hours, fifty-five minutes, and ten seconds had beaten that of Spirodon Lewes, who set his marathon record at the first modern Olympics the year before, the crowd proclaimed him the world champion.

The Boston Marathon has continued to grow in stature, but the Dartmouth Street Park did not remain as part of its story. Officials moved the finish line the following year.

An epilogue to the Dartmouth Street Grounds is recorded nearly forty years later, however. In 1934 the Boston Trojans of the American Basketball League, which had started life at Boston Arena, were forced to move

---

THE BOSTON MARATHON

The Boston Marathon was born as a direct result of the first modern Olympic Games, held at Athens in 1896. The Boston Athletic Association was well represented at those games. Association officials were so taken with the dramatic finish of the marathon in Greece that they decided to import the event to America. The inaugural run, which took place a few months later, in 1897, began at Metcalfe's Mill in Ashland, west of Boston, and finished at the Irvington Street Oval, site of the Dartmouth Street Grounds. Although the start and finish lines have moved, the Boston Marathon continues today, having been run more than one hundred times.

on. As bills for the fledgling team mounted, it could no longer afford the rent at the premier indoor venue in town, and thus turned to a more economical site. (For more information on the Boston Trojans, see pp. 81–82.) The Trojans finished their short sporting life at the Irvington Street Armory, executing jump shots and steals on what once had been the outfield of the Boston Unions.

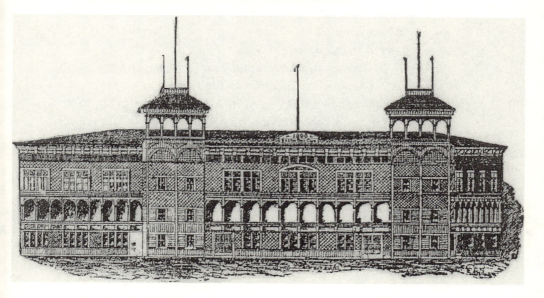

OPENED: April 3, 1890

CLOSED: June 30, 1894

CAPACITY: 20,000

TENANTS:

Boston Reds (Players League/American Association); *baseball, 1890 to 1891*

Boston Beaneaters (National League); *baseball, 1894 (temporary home)*

The Congress Street Grounds came into existence chiefly due to a movement among ballplayers who wanted greater control over their careers. A new league formed, which in turn allowed for the creation of a new Boston team, and with it, a new baseball venue. The park did not survive long, but in its short life considerable history took place within its walls, both on the field and in the boardroom.

In 1890, for the second time in seven years the reserve clause of the so-called national agreement leagues (National League and American Association) was challenged by the formation of a new organization. In 1884 the Union Association had tried and failed. Now the Players League would make the attempt. (For more information on the Union Association, see pp. 122–23.) This new group, also called at times the "Brotherhood League," included the players as full partners. At the end of the season, all revenues, minus expenses and salaries, were divided equally. The investors received 50 percent, while team members divided the other half among themselves.

As was the case in the UA of seven years earlier, the new Players League also had a Boston franchise. During that era, as in many years since, the Hub was well-known for drawing the best baseball crowds, and no new venture wanted to miss an opportunity to tap into Bostonians' enthusiasm for the sport.

A BOSTON HOME FOR THE PLAYERS LEAGUE

The National League, which dominated professional baseball, was not to be angered earlier than necessary; as the established baseball organization, it wielded considerable clout. Since the Players League planned to recruit much of its talent from among the stars in the National League, it wanted to keep its intentions quiet for as long as possible. John Morrill, representing the new Boston team, was sent in secret to scout out a site for a playing field. In October 1889 he reported to potential backers that two locations had proved satisfactory. His first choice was a site on Huntington Avenue, while a backup was found on newly created land in South Boston. The Commonwealth Flats sandbar had been covered with fill, turning it into a peninsula of solid land jutting into Boston Harbor.

The Players League held an organizing meeting on November 4, which included money men from Boston. Among them were former

(overleaf) FIGURE 46: Main entrance to the Congress Street Grounds, from Congress Street. The inscription in the middle reads, "1890 Boston Baseball Club."

130   *Reprinted with permission of the* Boston Herald

THE NATIONAL AGREEMENT

For the first six years of its existence, the National League had a monopoly on big-league professional baseball. That ended with the 1882 formation of a second major league, the American Association. After considerable thought as to how best to combat the newcomers, President Abraham Mills of the National League decided on a course of peaceful coexistence. A "national agreement" was drawn up and signed by all major and minor leagues, pledging respect for the contracts of each of the organizations. They agreed not to attempt the signing of players already under contract with any team in any of the leagues. In 1884 the agreement resulted in a post-season play-off series between pennant winners, for the national championship.

In later years, such leagues as the Union Association and Players League opted not to sign the agreement, resulting in considerable player raiding. After the demise of the Players League in 1891, when the spoils were divided between the remaining major leagues, disagreements resulted in the withdrawal of the American Association from the agreement.

mayor Frederick Prince; the ubiquitous Arthur Dixwell, a wealthy baseball fanatic; and George Wright, former Boston National League player and once an investor in the defunct Union Association. Ten days later the stockholders in the Boston team voted to accept Morrill's Huntington Avenue recommendation and a contingent of investors set off to inspect the grounds. At the site both good and bad points were discussed, and the trip was followed by a courtesy and curiosity visit to the rejected South Boston site. While there, the men began to rethink their decision.

The South Boston location on Congress Street offered room for a larger park, and a cool ocean breeze would be constant, even during the hottest summer months. It was also convenient to South Station for train service. John Montgomery Ward, league secretary and one of the driving forces behind the movement, preferred the Congress Street site because of its proximity to the financial district. He felt it was convenient for the businessmen to walk across the Congress Street Bridge from State Street. On the other hand, according to the *Boston Globe*, "Some of the stockholders felt that ladies might not go over there" since the area was considered dirty and dusty. In response, Arthur Irwin, future shortstop for the team and player representative, said, "Where one woman might be lost, six men would be added" (November 5, 1889).

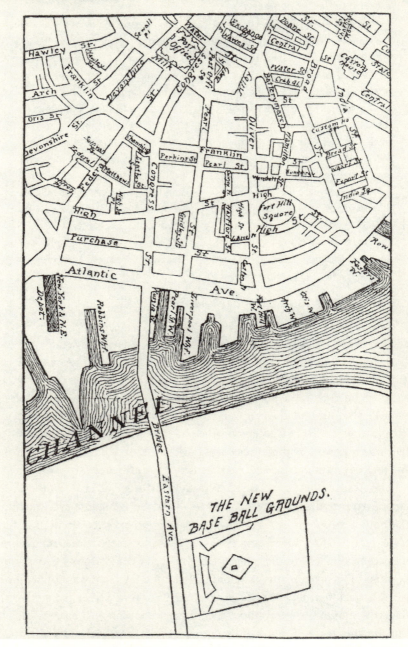

FIGURE 47: Newspaper map showing the location of the Congress Street Grounds. Although the map shows "Eastern Avenue," that piece of the road was known as Congress Street; *Boston Globe*, 1889. *Reprinted courtesy of* The Boston Globe

On December 10 the league signed a five-year lease agreement with the Boston Wharf Company, owners of the 200,000-square-foot Congress Street site, with an option to renew for an additional five years. The piece of land measured 350 feet along Congress Street, and 640 feet long, toward the harbor, making it considerably larger than the National League South End Grounds. Initially the plan was to model a new stadium after the Polo Grounds, home of the New York Giants, but architect M. B. Safford eventually built something original, using the attributes of the site to determine the final product.

In April 1890, the Congress Street Grounds welcomed the public to a park featuring a double-decked main pavilion 203 feet long and 62 feet wide, accommodating four thousand people. Under the stands were the ticket offices. The front of the structure, with two main entrances, was delineated at either end with 75-foot towers, each 25 feet square. The towers contained broad staircases leading to the first and second tiers of seats. (The park also had an elevator, reaching as high as the second tier.) Above the second tier and level with the roofline was an open balcony, where a band would play music during big events. On other days, additional seating could be placed there. At the top of each tower was a view of the harbor. On April 19 the *Boston Herald* wrote, "Ladies need not be debarred this luxury, as an easy flight of stairs communicates with the same, while the more adventuresome, with the sterner sex to accompany them, can attain to the highest pinnacle."

Atop the front of the building a plaque read "1890." Below it was a row of windows, below that was a set of ten archways, and below the archways was the street level. Situated on the two towers were flagpoles, flying the pennants of the teams in-house on game days. Weather flags were also flown, informing patrons of the status of the game during potential rain-outs. Angling back from the towers were the structure's sides, covering the backs of the grandstand. Each side contained an additional entrance. One flight above the street, and level with the first tier of seats, were two sets of rest rooms. Between the first and second tier were the players' dressing rooms, a practice hall (measuring 25 feet by 80 feet), a pressroom, the director's office, and telephone and telegraph equipment.

The structure and surrounding fence were painted in bright colors. The field itself was covered with a three-inch layer of coal cinders, rolled down hard and topped with rich loam. The infield was sod, and the outfield dirt. The distance from home plate to the center-field wall was considerably longer than the same measurement at the South End park.

"HI HI" DIXWELL

Among the most interesting of all Boston sports fans has to be General Arthur "Hi Hi" Dixwell. His unusual nickname comes from a cheer he made famous as he followed his favorite teams across the nation. Dixwell, who lived alone at his Copley Square Hotel apartment, was the ultimate baseball fan, or "crank," as they were known in that era, and traveled with the team on many of its road trips.

He seems to have been present at all the great sporting events in the city from the late 1800s to his death in 1924. He was sitting with Conant, the Braves owner, on the day the South End Grounds burned. He helped open the Congress Street Grounds as well as those at Huntington Avenue. For the latter park he turned the first shovelful of dirt at the groundbreaking ceremonies, and tossed out the first ball. Still later he was quoted in the newspaper at Cy Young's perfect game. "Never heard of such a performance. I have followed the game many years," he said.

He promoted an eccentric view of himself, always seen in colorful clothing and making offbeat remarks. Once he was reported as "looking the picture of the exiled President of the Transvaal." Other times the newspapers commented on his colorful vests. At the end of the 1890 season, he announced that for the following year he was seriously thinking of doing his "Hi Hi" cheer in German to waltz music.

Players knew Dixwell and liked him. Once in Cleveland he remained up all night just to get a glimpse of catcher Buck Ewing. As Ewing arrived at the hotel and stepped from his carriage, Dixwell, according to the *Globe*, "let out a Hi Hi that shook the ceiling" (*Boston Globe*, March 11, 1890).

In 1890, during one of his many trips, he stopped in on a series of negotiations between the National and Players Leagues and sent the results back to Boston. The reports ended when the chairman of the meeting had him removed. After his last correspondence, the *Boston Globe* observed, "General Dixwell, with a disconsolate look upon his chubby face, said it had been resolved to allow only delegates to remain" (March 12, 1890).

Once in a game at Buffalo he narrowly escaped removal from the stands, and possible arrest. The *Boston Globe* reported that throughout the first innings Dixwell continuously indulged in a chorus of "Hi Hi," until confronted by the local police. He was ordered to stop at once. Quite upset, Dixwell responded by saying, "Will the cheering keep the policeman on his beat?" As the police officer pressed the issue the team owner tried to intervene by saying, "The general is all right." The officer was not appeased. Although in Buffalo, the fans took up the Bostonian's cause and began chanting "Hi Hi," until the policeman gave up his quest, and left the bleachers to the cheering of the Buffalo partisans (*Boston Globe*, October 1, 1890).

Charles Sleeper and J. W. Wheeler immortalized Arthur Dixwell in a song. It was appropriately titled "Hi Hi," and respectfully dedicated to the general, as well as to the Players League.

First stanza:

We're out to win the pennant and we're styled the Players League.
 Our play is quite athletic and we
  never mind fatigue.
The ladies all applaud us and the
 cranks, they go insane.
The boys upon the bleaching boards
 are with us once again.

Chorus:

 Hi Hi, Hi Hi, solid strong and good.
Our ranks are filled with veterans.
 We're the National Brotherhood.

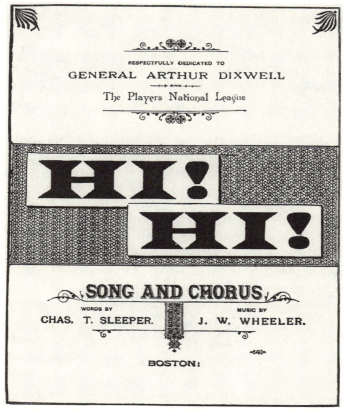

FIGURE 48: Title page of sheet music, dedicated to baseball fan Arthur Dixwell and the Players' National League, whose home in Boston was the Congress Street Grounds; 1890. *Reprinted courtesy of* The Boston Globe

ANIMOSITY ERUPTS

As the new league—and the potential for teams being fielded in both leagues in the same city—became reality, the gloves came off. The new Players League landed such stars as King Kelly and more than a hundred others. The National League fought back and offered bonuses to some if they returned. In response, Secretary Brunell published a scathing letter in the *New York Times*: "The Players League is now ready to begin the season with the strongest group of eight clubs ever gathered in one baseball organization. The [PL] men have withstood National League bombs, beaten the old masters in the court, rejected huge bribes, and defeated National League plots. There are 120 men loyal and true under contract today." His letter finished by saying, "It is very important that all offers from the bribers go before the public through the newspapers. Please see that they are fully exposed if they attempt to bribe you" (*New York Times*, February 27, 1890).

On March 11, 1890, the Players League published its schedule, with Boston slated to open at home on April 21. Two weeks later the National League met and finalized its own schedule, which contained fifty-eight conflicting dates (where two Boston teams would be home at the same time). Opening day was scheduled for April 19, two days before the PL teams were to begin play. The *Globe* reported that the National League magnates had no plans to work out the conflicts: "We shall not change our policy, shall ignore the Brotherhood, and proceed as if they did not exist." The *Boston Globe* asked Director Hart of Boston's PL team for a response, to which he stated, "Well if they can stand it, I guess we can, and I think they will get the worst of it. I am writing to John Ward [league secretary] now and I shall suggest that we open the season Saturday, April 19, the same day as the [National] League, and that will make 59 conflicting dates."

With the rivals virtually at war both nationally and locally, the new team went south for spring training. As the players headed for Savannah—with the band playing "Long Live the King" for local star King Kelly—work on the Congress Street Grounds proceeded through a series of snowstorms.

When the team pulled into Richmond it met up with the Quakers of the National League. On the Quakers were five men who had initially signed with the Players League, but eventually returned to their original team; the Brotherhood players viewed them as deserters. On Monday, March 24, the *Boston Globe* reported, "As the engine whistled coming into the depot, the Players League men lined up to view the men who left them. One of the young Philadelphians caught sight of the Boston players and passed the word down the straggling line. The Bostons stood like statues, with their eyes fixed on the old players. Big Sam Thompson was the first to pass. He looked at the familiar faces of his old comrades and reddened upon getting no sign of recognition. Clements looked up and then down like a man who had lost his way. Schriver turned all sorts of colors and kept his eyes on the ground. Myers, who had his wife with him, looked at the line of familiar faces and wilted. Gleason tried to smile, but the cold stare was too much, and his head twisted as if the air was hard to breathe. It was a sight never to be forgotten. The Boston players never made a sound but spoke volumes in looks."

THE NEW PARK OPENS

In early April the team returned home, where it would play its final warm-up games. The first event at the nearly completed Congress Street Grounds took place on Fast Day, once a holiday in Massachusetts. Adding fuel to the bitter rivalry, the National League Braves also played its exhibition game at the same time—the first of many direct confrontations.

Thursday, April 3, 1890, a large crowd was expected at the new park, and extra cars were put on the trains to accommodate the anticipated influx of business. Owners hoped for a crowd of 6,000, but the turnout exceeded 20,000. At the other end of town the Braves played a double-header in front of only 3,967. At Congress Street a police detail of ten had been ordered, but was doubled an hour before game time. By the opening pitch it had been doubled again, and doubled once more during the afternoon.

FAST DAY BASEBALL

Beginning in the 1870s Fast Day was the traditional date for Boston baseball teams to begin their preliminary games after returning from spring training. Fast Day, originally intended for religious observances, fell on the first Thursday in April. Many people had the day off from work, giving the parks a good chance at a large crowd.

In the 1890s the holiday disappeared when the more popular and secular Patriot's Day, held on April 19, took its place. To this day, the Patriot's Day game is special for the Red Sox. Play starts in the morning so that the last out will be made in time for the Fenway faithful to spill into Kenmore Square to see the marathoners go by.

As the crowd gathered at the park, a selected group from the Brotherhood took on the task of greeting the players of the two opposing teams. Coaches and landaus were lined up in front of the Tremont House, and a parade, under the direction of the Elks Club, wound its way through the city and eventually to Congress Street. Waiting outside the park were about ten thousand fans who had not been able to gain admission, but were on hand to welcome King Kelly and John Montgomery Ward as conquering heroes.

Inside was a wild scene, with spectators found everywhere. Not only had all available room in the unfinished grandstand been taken up, but the crowd also had spilled into the outfield. People were lined up against the fences on all sides; the rooftops of nearby buildings were full, as was the nearby grain elevator—until being cleared by a fire hose. Many baseball fans climbed on top of rail cars stored behind center field. The *Boston Herald* declared it the largest crowd ever assembled to witness an exhibition game, and the largest the city had ever seen for any game. According to the *Boston Post*, "[A] large gate was broken down by the crowd and fully five hundred persons gained free admittance" (April 4, 1890). Thousands of fans were turned away.

No real baseball playing could take place as there was little room left in the outfield. It was only an exhibition game, though, and those in attendance appeared not to mind.

FINISHING TOUCHES

Following the first home game, management scrambled to complete the park. Workers finished all grandstand seats (built by the Grand Rapids Furniture Company) and installed five thousand additional "bleaching benches" in center field. The new capacity cut down the size of the outfield, however, and all balls hit over the closer fence would be ruled as doubles, much to the vexation of the players.

While the Congress Street Grounds were being completed, huge crowds welcomed Boston's Players League club throughout Massachusetts, where it played the remaining exhibition games in Lowell, Taunton, and other suburban cities.

As April 19 approached, the city buzzed with anticipation. The National League team was considered a favorite for the pennant, and the new Players League contingent could possibly have put together the best side in the nation. Both teams had built a loyal following, despite the newness of the Players League. The night before opening day the *Globe* declared that "never before had there been such a deep interest shown in the national game." About five hundred people toured the new grounds on Congress Street, inspecting the major changes that had been implemented since the Fast Day exhibition. All the center-field bleachers were complete, and the remaining grandstand seats were in place, covered by a roof. Ornamental metal slate, alternated with spruce bracketing in many colors, had been installed. A few carpenters remained, putting the finishing touches on the gingerbread work in the grandstand.

VICTORY ON THE FIELD AND AT THE BOX OFFICE

On opening day the two Boston teams were ready for a showdown, although neither team would play the other; their battle was waged at the box office and in the boardroom. Visiting the National League Braves at the South End was Brooklyn of that league. At the new Congress Street park another Brooklyn team was also in town for the season opener. Two "burgees," or flags, flew high over the stadium, announcing the matchup: the Brooklyn pennant was white, with the word "Brooklyn" in blue, representing the team colors; the home flag, also white, had the word "Boston" in red. With full pricing in place for league games, the crowds at both parks were down a bit from the earlier matches. The South End turnstile registered three thousand fans, while at Congress Street, ten thousand showed up to cheer on the Brotherhood.

At about 2 P.M. Congress Street was crowded with fans from the park, stretching back to the Fort Point Channel. Scalpers were seen at the bridge and all the way down Congress Street. Prices ranged from sixty cents to seventy-five cents. A man set up an unofficial concession stand, selling food and drink to those waiting to reach the stadium. Inside, the strains of Reeves' American Band, from Providence, entertained those lucky enough to be seated already. In the grandstand one of the fans held an impromptu "meeting of the supporters." According to the *Boston Herald*, they voted to rename themselves. Doing away with the old baseball term "crank," they would henceforth be known as "Brotherites," honoring the Brotherhood League.

The game was nearly an anticlimax as the partylike atmosphere was foremost a celebration of the league. In any case, Boston's 3–2 win over the highly touted Brooklyn nine boded well for a successful season.

The Players League's dominance at the gate continued through the first week as the new team racked up an average attendance of 3,751 while the National League counterpart totaled only 1,759. As the season wore on, the numbers got closer, but the Congress Street contingent held the lead. By September Boston's PL team led its own league, and all of 139 professional baseball, with an average attendance of 2,705. The Boston Nationals were second in their league only to Philadelphia, which sold tickets for half the price. Combined, the city far outstripped its closest counterparts in attendance.

Although the older National League Braves maintained a loyal following, the city's Players League team captured the imaginations of the Boston sports fans. Three reasons seem to account for the instant loyalty. First, the Players League had managed to sign many of the game's best and most colorful players, including King Kelly, possibly the most well known player, who had abandoned the Boston Braves, and signed on with the new club. Secondly, the new Boston team had built a strong contender. In fact, many sportswriters from across the country proclaimed it the best team in any of the existing leagues. Finally, the new Congress Street Grounds were larger, more comfortable, and much more modern than the old South End Grounds.

The National League Braves finished the season twelve games off the top, but the new Brotherhood team was extremely successful in its inaugural campaign. Boston won the championship by six and a half games over their opening-day rivals from Brooklyn, stacking up a record of eighty-one wins to 48 losses.

Two great parties fêted the conquering heroes. The first took place at the Congress Street Grounds on Saturday, October 11, with an exhibition game against New York. It was followed by a base-running contest featuring Tom Brown and Harry Stovey, a ball-throwing match between Ed Crane and Harry Vaughan, and the presentation of the pennant by league president McAlperin. King Kelly raised the flag up a brand-new pole, erected for the occasion, and Reeves' American Band once

---

FORT POINT CHANNEL

The Fort Point Channel area has always been considered a prime location for sports venues. In the 1960s the South Station neighborhood was included in plans for a multisport complex, housing both football and baseball. Again in the 1990s the area was examined by the New England Patriots for the construction of a Fox-boro Stadium replacement. Even the Red Sox thought the site—with its close proximity to Boston's downtown area—might suit their purposes. These baseball and football parks, proposed but never realized, would have included parts of the Congress Street Grounds site.

again entertained the crowd. The second half of the celebration took place the next evening in the Grand Sacred Concert at the Music Hall in downtown Boston. Featured performers, according to an advertisement in the *Boston Globe*, were De Wolf Hopper of De Wolf Hopper's Opera Company, W. H. MacDonald of the Bostonian Opera Company, vaudeville acts, the Olympia and Harlem Quartets, an Electric Banjo and Guitar Quartet, and the Grand Orchestra under the direction of John C. Mullay.

THE LEAGUE DIES BUT THE TEAM SURVIVES

Before the number of major leagues was reduced to two in 1891 and finally to one in 1892, owners of various leagues tussled for survival on the field, at the box office, and in backroom negotiations. Despite the Players League's excellent season and its enormous popularity with the fans, it was not able to withstand the economic power wielded by the establishment, and it died. The Players League's Boston franchise was not ready to give up so easily.

Following a winter of negotiations, the Boston Braves made peace with their crosstown rivals, but on National League terms. The NL agreed to allow the local Players League team to join the American Association if it met certain criteria: The owner had to agree that his team would abide by the reserve clause. The price of admission had to remain at fifty cents, even though most Association teams charged only a quarter. The National League would play on Decoration Day, May 30, and the Association would have the Fourth of July. Finally, the Association team had to pick a distinct name; the term "Boston," henceforth was to refer to the NL team only. Boston's PL team agreed to all demands; it joined the American Association as the "Reds" and the Players League passed into history.

Despite all the concessions, on April 3, 1891, Boston's two teams again went head-to-head. As was the case the previous season, the new team was the victor in terms of ticket sales. The National League, playing at the South End Grounds, garnered the support of 6,155 faithful fans, but were outdone by the Reds at Congress Street. They sold 7,412 tickets.

A STREETCAR SERIES?

The Reds in their second season and their second league were as successful as they had been the year before. They led most of the way, dropping out of first place on only two brief occasions, and won the American Association pennant by three and a half games. Their closest rival was 141

Chicago, which was also a refugee from the Players League. At the end of the fourth inning on October 3, General Dixwell gave a short speech and presented the championship flag. As the pennant went up the pole the crowds cheered and the players waved their caps. As luck would have it the Boston Braves also won, topping the National League—beating out St. Louis by eight and a half games.

This turn of events appeared to set the stage for a major showdown on the diamond. Since 1884 the champions of the two big leagues had squared off in a series to determine the World Championship. With both local teams winning, Bostonians were gearing up for the first "streetcar series."

The playoffs in 1891 were no sure thing, however. During the season a break had occurred between the two remaining major leagues and the national agreement was disbanded. Apparently because two former Players League teams had been allowed to join the American Association, the National League felt that it had been cheated out of its players who had signed with the Players League the year before. On October 8, 1891, the management of the Boston Reds received a telegram from Association headquarters, authorizing it to challenge the Boston Braves to a best-of-five-games series. The National League office sent the following reply:

> I hold in my possession an agreement called the National Agreement which was solemnly signed by three parties, one of which was your association. I sincerely regret that the breaking of that agreement by your association renders such a series as you propose, impossible.

The series between the two leagues would never take place. Within a month, the end of the American Association was at hand. A league conference was held in New York on October 12 at which a new twelve-

---

THE SUCCESSFUL 1890S

The baseball world centered on Boston in the 1890s. The city won the National League pennant five times: 1891, 1892, and 1893 and then again in 1897 and 1898. The Reds took the title in 1890, winning the only Players League flag ever offered, and followed up with the last American Association title, in 1891. Ironically, a century later, in the 1990s, the city of Boston would go through its first decade without a league championship in any professional sport.

team circuit was proposed. The plan was to take four top teams from the Association, add them to the eight already in the National League, and split into two divisions. Within weeks the plan was put in place. The Boston Reds did not survive to enter the National League. Their franchise and player contracts were bought by the Braves, and they were shut down. The baseball war in Boston had ended and an even stronger local National League team went on to win the next two pennants.

LIFE AFTER THE REDS

The Congress Street Grounds remained without a professional baseball team for two years, until disaster struck at the South End Grounds. In a devastating fire on May 15, 1894, the park was leveled. The blaze started during the third inning of a game between Boston and Baltimore. (For more information on the stadium fire, see pp. 15–19.) The teams hardly missed a beat, however, as the club secured a one-month lease on the idle field in South Boston. During the National League's very short tenure at the site, some significant history was made. By the time a surreal May 30 double-header was completed, a record was set that major leaguers are still trying to beat more than a century later.

The first game of the double-header against Cincinnati was played on a cold, rainy morning before three thousand fans. Boston won the slugfest 13–10. It is the second game, however, that lives on in the history books. The skies cleared, but the afternoon was still fairly chilly. The park jutted out into the harbor, subjecting it to a stiff ocean breeze and mist. With the slight improvement in the weather the crowd swelled a bit to thirty-five hundred. Elton "Iceberg" Chamberlain was pitching for Cincinnati when Boston second baseman Bobby Lowe put his mark indelibly on the game of baseball. In his second at-bat he singled, but for the rest of the afternoon he hit nothing but home runs. In all, he would round the bases four times. At each successive trip to the plate the crowd cheered louder. According to the *Boston Globe*, "[E]ven the visitors had smiles on their faces." The feat had never been accomplished before, and they all knew they were witness to something special. Together with his single he had earned a total of seventeen bases, which also stood as a record. Although this total has been tied more than a dozen times since, no one—through the end of the twentieth century and into the twenty-first century, had bested the mark of four home runs in a game.

A legend states that one of the four-baggers hit at Congress Street is to this day the longest ever hit. As the story goes, the ball cleared the center-field fence, landed in an open railroad car, and was discovered several days later in Chicago.

The last game played at Congress Street was on June 20, 1894, when the Braves defeated Baltimore 14–12 in front of 2,091 fans. Those in attendance included many followers of the old American Association, on hand for a final afternoon of baseball at their park. The NL team moved back to the rebuilt South End Grounds, where Bobby Lowe finished the season with a total of eleven home runs.

The park at South Boston had a very short life. According to insurance maps of the area, the site appears with no ballpark just five years after its construction. The 1899 map depicts only a small shed at the edge of the street where the field once stood. By 1901 the entire east side of Congress Street was populated with commercial buildings, and was crossed by Pittsburgh (today Thompson) and Stillings Streets. No signs remain of the field that housed a two-time, two-league pennant winner. Its perfect record made it the most successful, albeit short-lived, professional franchise in baseball history.

12

WORCESTER COUNTY AGRICULTURAL FAIRGROUNDS

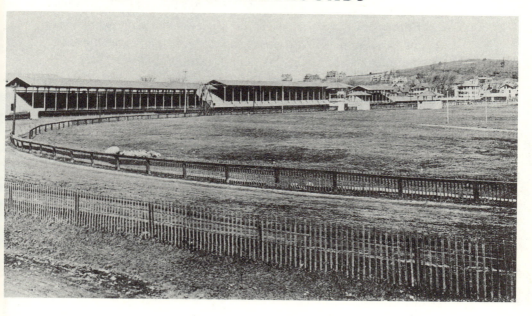

OPENED: 1853

CLOSED: 1898

CAPACITY: 4,000 (approximately)

TENANT:

Worcesters Baseball (National Association); *baseball, 1879*
(National League); *baseball, 1880–1883*

The Worcesters of central Massachusetts were members of the National League for three years, and played at what may have been the oddest park the major leagues have ever seen. The Worcester County Agricultural Fairgrounds—boasting ruts and holes left over from tractor-pulling competitions, and a tree growing in left field—was often the butt of jokes from visiting press. In reality the park was not built for baseball, but rather was the site of Worcester's annual September agricultural fair. In addition to the traditional attractions, the grounds also boasted such events as cricket and rugby matches.

Originally purchased by the County Agricultural Society in 1853, it also served as a training and recruiting camp for Union soldiers during the Civil War. Afterwards it continued its purpose as a fairground until the society moved to another site in 1898.

Today no traces of the park exist. The area is now partially covered by Becker College, and a plaque on the campus grounds helps keep its baseball past alive.

WORCESTER IN THE MINORS

In 1879 the Worcester Baseball Association was formed and placed a team in the minor league National Association, consisting of clubs from Albany, Washington, Holyoke, Springfield, New Bedford, Rochester, and Utica. Under the presidency of Worcester's former mayor Charles Pratt, the organization set out to construct a competitive squad from the top down. It eyed Frank Bancroft, known as "the prince of managers," for the top slot. Bancroft, in turn, wanted to sign Lee Richmond, a pitching sensation at Brown University. At first Richmond ignored Bancroft's overtures, not wanting to forfeit his amateur status and risk his spot on the Brown University team. Eventually the manager talked him into starting an exhibition game against National League champion, Chicago. Richmond sparkled, tossing a no-hitter in his first professional game. He was convinced to join the team after that.

Arthur Irwin signed on as shortstop, and popular "Chub" Sullivan took over at first base. Sullivan, a crowd favorite, was viewed as somewhat of a clown. He was also an early pioneer of the slide.

The Worcesters leased the Agricultural Fairgrounds, paying five hundred dollars for the year, which gave them complete control of the

(overleaf) FIGURE 49: Grandstand at the Worcester Fairground, ca. 1880.

From the collections of WORCESTER HISTORICAL MUSEUM, Worcester, MA.

event schedule for the park. The grounds, bounded by Sever, Cedar, Highland, and Agricultural Streets, were ringed with a half-mile horse track. The baseball diamond was placed in the middle. Behind the backstop was a scorer's stand; a wooden grandstand, used primarily for the track, paralleled the first-base line. Carriages could be driven in and parked along the track, affording a much better view. According to Worcester baseball historian Brian Goslow, fans in the carriages often became part of the action as "umpires sometimes took testimony from spectators to settle disputed calls."

As the first season opened, large banners depicting a batter at the plate adorned lampposts throughout downtown. Scores were sent to the *Worcester Telegram* office, where they were posted; a scoreboard stood in front of the Friendly Clothing Store on Main Street, as well. New England Telephone provided a service that was revived by its successor firm 120 years later: for twenty-five cents a person not able to get to the park could subscribe to a plan in which scores and game summaries were provided by telephone.

While the team played in the National Association women were encouraged to attend, and were allowed into the Worcester park free of charge. The *Worcester Daily Spy* reported, "The presence of ladies in the grandstand and carriages outside the track, gives character to the sport." This practice caused trouble at the end of the season during exhibition games with National League teams. The Association rules stipulated that the visiting club should receive half of the twenty-five cent admission price for every person in the park. When Cincinnati came to town, the team insisted on its full share per person, regardless of whether or not all of the people in the stands had paid. Upon hearing this, Harry Wright of Boston, whose team had just visited Worcester, said he had not realized the policy. Since there was no way of knowing the number of women who had been in attendance, he would not insist on the extra money for the game already played, but would do so in the future.

According to contemporary accounts, the Worcester team members were gentlemanly, but apparently the clientele in the stands was not. Gambling and drinking created problems. Brian Goslow wrote that in one game "[a] man was thrown headlong down the seats, and another had his head mashed with a bottle." Because of these incidents the league prohibited the sale of liquor and the practice of betting within the park perimeter during games.

FIGURE 50: Poster for the Worcesters of the National League, depicting the manager and players, 1879. *National Baseball Hall of Fame Library, Cooperstown, N.Y.*

EXHIBITION GAMES

As the first season neared its close, the Worcesters had the opportunity to play against stronger competition. By entering the New England Championship tournament, they were pitted against such regional rivals in the National League as Boston and Providence. In extra matches, they also played Chicago and Cincinnati, faring quite well against representatives of the more-established league. In the period between September 22 and October 3, Worcester beat the 1878 champions from Boston twice, and the soon-to-be pennant winners from Providence, once.

After the game with the Rhode Island team in Worcester, the *Providence Journal* provoked a rivalry by blaming the loss on the condition of the grounds, pointing out that it was rutted and hilly. The paper stated, "Providence would win on a field with proper fence boundaries." It also referred to the Worcester team as "semi-professional."

On October 12 Providence had its shot at revenge, as a return match was scheduled for its own Messer Street Grounds. Unfortunately for Providence, things did not go its way in the second game, either. Worcester won the game by a score of 3–2. The *Worcester Daily Spy* took the opportunity to rub salt in the wound. "At a game in Providence, after many days of impatient waiting, 1200 Providence people saw the Providence Nine get the semi-pros from Worcester on a ground with proper fence boundaries, free from precipice banks, and breakneck holes." The *Spy* got in one more dig, noting that the Providence park "is too small for a proper game" (October 12, 1879).

The banter between newspapers continued with the *Journal* saying that the Worcester ballground "was a rough broken field remarkable for its pits and mounds, perfect traps for the unacquainted." The paper facetiously said, "Outfielder Paul Hines was last seen knee deep in a hole chasing a fly ball."

Despite problems with an inferior park, the first year had been a success. The team earned a strong 81–42 record, including exhibition matches. Against the National League clubs, they went a respectable

---

THE TEAM'S NAME

Although history books often refer to them as the "Brown Stockings" or "Ruby Legs," the name of the team was simply the "Worcesters." Bill Ballou of the *Worcester Telegram* researched all contemporary accounts of the team and has found no other reference. The term "Brown Stockings" apparently comes from the write-up of the team on opening day, describing the white flannel uniforms, "Chicago-style" caps, brown stockings, and leather shoes. The socks are never mentioned again. Historian Brian Goslow feels that the term "Ruby Legs" was ascribed to the team erroneously. A headline once read "Ruby Legs Defeat Worcester." "Ruby Legs" in that instance seems to refer to the Boston team, whose signature uniform included red stockings.

6–5. They had also managed to show a profit. With such positive results in hand, and despite being only forty miles west of Boston, the team decided to make a jump to the National League. The Syracuse Stars of that organization had faltered during the season and were now gone. A replacement club was needed and Worcester hoped to get the nod. Stiff competition was evident from Washington and Albany, however. While the board of directors awaited a decision on their petition, Manager Frank Bancroft took the team on a training tour of Cuba. Temporarily playing under the name "Hop Bitters," Worcester fared well on the road.

JOINING THE NATIONAL LEAGUE

On Saturday, February 7, 1880, the *Worcester Spy* reported that the local team had received admission to the National League, by a vote of six to one. Changes were made to strengthen the team, but for the most part the same set of players from the successful 1879 season were back in uniform. Manager Frank Bancroft received a lucrative offer from the Crescent Citys of New Orleans to take over their club, but decided instead to guide Worcester into the National League. Their playing field, often called the "driving park" due to the enclosing horse track, was improved slightly, as a newly painted white fence was erected. The *Chicago Tribune* had high hopes for the new entrant, picking it for second place, behind only Providence and ahead of its own home team.

To develop a treasury for operating expenses, the Worcester Baseball Club held fund-raising events at Mechanics Hall. Included were a series of ten-mile walking matches and a five-mile running race. Door prizes included a season ticket to the ball grounds. Tickets could also be purchased at special low rates at the hall.

THE PRICE OF ADMISSION

One of the conditions set by the National League for Worcester's entry into the majors was an agreement on ticket prices. Worcester, when playing in the minor league, had charged twenty-five cents for admission. In order to play in the National League they would have to double the price. Many felt that the price hike was financial suicide, but the local press supported the increase. The *Worcester Spy* felt that some patronage might be lost, but most would be willing to pay a higher price for better-quality baseball. The team's board of directors agreed, and admission to the National League was granted.

THE 1880 SEASON

The first season in the major league was a success. The team did not do as well as the Chicago paper had predicted, but there were enough highlights to keep press and fan support on the side of the club.

The Worcesters reached their absolute peak on June 12, 1880. Lee Richmond, the pitching phenomenon from Brown University, was engaged in pregraduation events in Providence the day before his big game. On the morning of the twelfth he caught a late train up to Worcester, arriving without even a chance to eat. At the fairgrounds he was pitted against Big Jim McCormick of Cleveland. By the end of the game, history had been written, forever making the inferior baseball field hallowed ground in baseball lore.

The game was a pitchers' duel from the outset. After three full innings no one from either club had reached first base. In the bottom of the fourth, Richmond was the first to break the ice, hitting a single off his rival. Throughout the rest of the game McCormick gave up only three additional hits and allowed just one run. Richmond, however, kept up his mastery. At the end of the eighth, no Cleveland runner had made it to first. Then Mother Nature stepped in—a quick rain shower delayed the game, adding to the tension and excitement. When play resumed, Richmond took up where he left off, retiring the final three batters. Richmond had been perfect. He threw the first of what he called a "no-hit, no-run, no man to reach first" game. There were seven hundred fans on hand to witness Richmond's third professional no-hitter and baseball's first perfect game.

Remarkably, five days after Lee Richmond performed the feat, Monty Ward of Providence threw baseball's second perfect game. There would not be another one until Cy Young's gem in the American League in 1904. (For more information on Cy Young's perfect game, see pp. 41–42.) In 1964, Jim Bunning pitched the next National League perfect game, eighty-four years after Richmond's performance.

On August 13 manager Bancroft tried a unique experiment in another game against Cleveland. Lee Richmond was baseball's first regular left-handed pitcher, and teams had begun to change rotations in order to adjust. In that game, Bancroft countered by swapping two pitchers on and off the mound. Richmond pitched to left-handed batters, while Fred Corey threw to right-handers. When not pitching, each would remain in the game by playing right field. The strategy worked: the Worcesters won 3–1. Worcester ended the season in a respectable fifth place.

FIGURE 51: Plaque at Becker College marking the site of the Worcester County Agricultural Fairgrounds and Lee Richmond's perfect game. The inscription reads, "On June 12, 1880, the first perfect game in professional baseball history was pitched on this site (the former Worcester Agricultural Fairgrounds) by J. Lee Richmond of Worcester against Cleveland in a National League game."
Courtesy of Dianne M. Foulds

THE 1881 SEASON

The team's second season in the majors was plagued by miscues and bad performance. Manager Frank Bancroft had moved on, replaced by Mike Dorgan. Dorgan was gone by August 18, with the reins being taken by Harry Stovey. The following day the team received a further blow; star shortstop Arthur Irwin broke his leg when he tripped rounding first. The team had an eight-run lead at the time. Lewis Dickerson, the logical replacement, was already out with injuries. With no backup in place the new manager took drastic action. According to historian Brian Goslow, Flip Flaherty, owner of a local sporting-goods store, was called out of the stands. He donned a uniform and finished the game. To make matters worse for both players and fans, rain began falling. With spirits low, the lead dissipated and the game ended in a tie. Less than a month later popular player Chub Sullivan died of tuberculosis. For the remainder of the season the Worcester players wore black armbands in mourning.

In September, charges were made against Worcester's Lip Pike. He had been suspected of throwing ball games in the past, but in a game against Boston, matters came to a head. The *Worcester Spy* wrote that Pike's "course led to the charge of crookedness as he walked after fumbled balls, threw to Bushong [the catcher] when ordered to throw to Creamer, and almost walked from first to second on a safe hit, on which he could easily have reached third" (September 5, 1881). By the end of the month the league expelled Pike.

In the fall, the western teams of the league began to talk as if Worcester would not be back the next year. Detroit in particular wanted the city replaced by one that would draw better crowds. With miniscule gate receipts, it was expensive for teams to travel there. The Worcester Baseball Association, however, wanted to dispel all rumors, and voted unanimously to continue.

THE LAST SEASON

The season of 1882 was even worse than the one previous. The pitchers complained of overwork, and the lack of wins seemed to prove their point. As the team sank further in the standings, the ever-dwindling crowds began to get hostile. At midseason the average attendance reached as low as fifty. The newspapers, which had been staunch defenders, were no longer as quick to overlook the team's defects. A game with Buffalo was referred to as an important match to determine last place. The Buffalo manager, James O'Rourke, went so far as to call it "the worst game ever played by a professional team" (*Worcester Gazette*, June 16, 1882).

Worcester went through three managers that season, and the league planned a meeting for September 22, 1882, to discuss the situation. As the fateful league meeting approached, rumors abounded that Worcester would be asked to leave—which they were, despite the fledgling team's objections. With money in short supply and with a terrible record of eighteen wins and sixty-six losses, Worcester finally resigned. After three tumultuous years in the National League, Worcester's days as a major league baseball city sputtered to an end.

At Worcester's first game following the vote to disband at the end of the season, attendance hit an all-time low. With Troy (New York) the other doomed team as their opponent, there were six paying customers in the stands. The next day, Worcester's last, there were twenty-five.

DID THE WORCESTER TEAM MOVE TO PHILADELPHIA?

Today's Philadelphia Phillies claim to be descendants of the Worcesters Baseball Club of the National League. The thread connecting the two teams is tenuous at best. The Worcester organization did not move, but rather was dissolved. There was no transfer of franchises either. When Troy and Worcester were dissolved, they were simply replaced by two new teams in New York and Philadelphia. The only connection lies in the fact that when one team left the league, the other took its place.

13

SAM MARK'S STADIUM

OPENED: September 24, 1922

CLOSED: Approximately 1950

CAPACITY: 15,000 (3,000 seated)

TENANTS:

Fall River Marksmen (American Soccer League); *soccer, 1922 to 1930*

Fall River Football Club (American Soccer League); *soccer, 1931*

The empty, overgrown field behind the Ponta Del Gada Club on Shove Street in Tiverton, Rhode Island, strikes one as an unlikely place to have once welcomed the great visiting soccer teams from Europe and South America and staged important cup finals. Sam Mark's Stadium served just that purpose, however, more than sixty years before "soccer moms" became a political force. The park was built to attract fans from Fall River, a city fifty miles south of Boston, but was located on a side street in an industrial section of nearby Tiverton, just across the state line in Rhode Island. Today, because of the condition of the field it's nearly impossible to imagine a soccer field at the site, but a sense of proportion and boundary can be discerned when comparing the vacant lot with photographs taken in the stadium's heyday. The mill building from the 1920s still stands behind it, as a backdrop; although now minus its once-grand clock tower, the aging relic serves as a landmark. The original smokestack of the mill still stands as well. The bumpy field remains empty, ringed with trees and low growth, eerily marking roughly where the overflowing grandstands stood. Surveying the scene today, one can almost imagine the partisan crowd cheering on their local team at the expense of the many well-known clubs from across the nation and around the world.

FALL RIVER JOINS THE MAJOR LEAGUES

In early 1922, sports promoter Sam Mark purchased a franchise in the one-year-old American Soccer League and set out to create a winner. Fall River had been a soccer hotbed for several years, developing considerable homegrown talent. Building around such locals as Albert Lynn and Hughie Weir, Mark also signed up big-time players from Europe.

Chief among the foreign talent was Harold Brittan, a center forward for the famed Chelsea Football (soccer) Club of England, playing for that team for seven years prior to his emigration. The *Fall River Globe* called him "the $10,000 soccer beauty"; in his six-year career in Fall River, he scored 103 times. He was regarded as the best forward in the United States.

In addition to building a championship contender, Mark set out to build a suitable home for his team. Nearly eight decades before the

(overleaf) FIGURE 52: The site of Sam Mark's Stadium in Tiverton, R.I., home of the Fall River Marksmen of the American Soccer League. Many famous teams from Europe played here, and the 1925 National Open Cup was won at the site, as Shawsheen beat the Chicago Canadians. *Courtesy of Dianne M. Foulds*

modern era of soccer-specific stadium building began in Columbus, Ohio, and Charleston, South Carolina, Fall River had a professional park constructed first and foremost for its local soccer franchise.

Location, Location, Location

Mark chose to build in Rhode Island because of the "blue laws" prevailing in Massachusetts at the time. Sunday games were not allowed in Fall River, but permits could easily be obtained in Tiverton. Mark's Stadium stood as close to Fall River as possible—the state and city line ran directly behind the north goal. Fall River's trolley line conveniently stopped very near the field entrance, simplifying transportation. The town of Tiverton and the state of Rhode Island welcomed the venue with open arms.

OPENING DAYS

After a series of false starts, the building of the stadium fell behind schedule. Originally slated for Sunday, September 17, 1922, the first game was put off for a week, and the official opening ceremony two weeks after that, to allow completion of construction. As steamrollers were brought in to put the playing field in shape on the morning of game day, the visiting Saylesville club of Pawtucket arrived. The stands were not yet ready and the enclosing fence was not completely built, but the rescheduled game went on anyway.

At 3 P.M. on Sunday, September 24, twenty-five hundred fans showed up to watch the new team in its new home. Unfortunately for the home crowd, the opponents scored three quick goals in the first half. Saving face, the Marksmen came back to tie it on goals by Brittan, Clark, and Rattigan. Despite its incomplete state, the new park was popular with the crowd.

The *Fall River Globe* gave both team and park rave reviews. "The demonstration in attendance for the game yesterday, a practice game only, amply implies how eager the public is for a Sunday diversion. The influx to the town over the border took place orderly and in a manner that reflects credit to Fall River Transportation" (September 25, 1922).

The second unofficial opening came a week later when the Paterson Football Club of New Jersey came to town. Although both teams were in the American Soccer League, the game was just a warm-up for real league action, scheduled to begin a week later. Mark announced that the field was in complete readiness except for the roof over the grandstand. Nearly three thousand people passed through the gates to watch the New

157

Jersey team win by a score of 3 to 0. The game showed up many weaknesses in Fall River's all-star lineup and Mark vowed to strengthen his club.

The official league opener coincided with the stadium's scheduled grand-opening celebration. Several events were planned, including a concert by Allston's twenty-piece band and a visit from the governors of both Rhode Island and Massachusetts, the mayor of Fall River, and selectmen of Tiverton, as well as league dignitaries. "Megaphone man" Eddie Bowden, hired to make announcements during the game, would be on hand to give the scores of baseball's World Series game being played the same day. The results would be coming hot off the wire.

Unfortunately none of the planned pomp took place. Ominous weather reports arrived throughout the morning, and everything but the game itself was canceled.

At precisely 3 o'clock, exactly when the visiting J & P Coats team was to enter the park, a torrential rainstorm began. The two thousand spectators sitting in the grandstand all ran for cover. The squall only lasted ten minutes, but it caused considerable damage. According to the *Fall River Globe*, "In the ten minute work-out Jupiter Pluvius had done his worst. The drains on the new field could not take care of the big volume of water in the short space of time" (October 9, 1922). The field was a sea of mud. Apparently the conditions did not bother the visitors as much as the Fall River team: J & P Coats took the match 1 to 0.

The Fall River Marksmen finished third that first season, losing to the champion Coats team as well as to Bethlehem Steel, but they came back strong in the sophmore year. Sam Mark's boys took the next three pennants, then repeated the feat again between 1928 and 1930.

NAMING OF THE STADIUM

On September 13, 1922, just days before the grand opening, owner Sam Mark announced a contest to choose a name for the brand-new park. The only requirements for entering the contest were that the submitter must be a resident of either Fall River or Tiverton, and the name should be as brief as possible. Sam Mark himself would present the winner with a twenty-dollar gold piece, and the person would take part in the dedication ceremony. Mark received more than twelve hundred entries, and declared Miss Annie Martin of Osborn Street, the winner. The name she chose? "Sam Mark's Stadium," of course.

In the ten years that the Marksmen played at Fall River, the team compiled an amazing record. Playing the best professional clubs in the nation, they won the league championship six times, and took the U.S. Open Cup three times. Top goal scorers were Harold Brittan, reaching as high as thirty-two goals one season, Tec White with thirty-three, and Bill McPherson.

FAMOUS GUESTS

In addition to league play, Mark's Stadium was the scene of many important matches. In April 1925 the park hosted the U.S. Open Cup final game, pitting the Shawsheen Indians against the Chicago Canadians. (For more information on the Shawsheen Indians and the Open Cup tournament, see chapter 14.) The tournament was open to all amateur and professional teams in the country, and Mark's Stadium was chosen as a neutral site. Since the city of Fall River had expected its team to win the cup that year and interest in the tournament ran high, Sam Mark offered his stadium for the title match, feeling that the city would support the game.

Many well-known teams showed up at the Shove Street park in Tiverton. Late in the first season, the Dick, Kerr Ladies Football Club from Newcastle, England, played an exhibition match. Although the score was 2 to 2, the newspapers reported that it was more of an unofficial exhibition than a real game. Throughout the decade the Marksmen played host to several international teams: Sparta of Greece, the Uruguay National Team, the Italian National Team, Glasgow Celtic, Kilmarnock, and Velee Sarsfield.

Fall River scored a major upset when playing the Glasgow Rangers on June 3, 1928. The Glasgow team, touted as the best European team ever to travel to the United States, was held scoreless by the locals at Mark's Stadium. A record crowd of 15,472 jammed every possible space at the park to see the famous club outplayed by Fall River.

On September 4, 1929, arc lights were introduced at Tiverton. The first night game was played there between Fall River and the Hakoah All-Stars, six years before major league baseball began playing under the lights.

THE STREAK ENDS

As the Great Depression set in, Sam Mark noticed a precipitous drop in attendance. There simply was not enough money available in the hard-hit Fall River area for people to purchase tickets. In February

1931, he regretfully made the decision to move his team to New York, and renamed it the New York Soccer Yankees. He offered the use of his stadium to anyone who wished to operate a new Fall River team. Harold Brittan, his star from the early days of the Marksmen, took him up on his offer. Buying the defunct Providence franchise in the American Soccer League, he moved into Sam Mark's Stadium with his Fall River Football Club. Brittan ran headlong into the problems that Mark had foreseen; his team lasted only one season.

In later years, the famed Fall River Ponta Del Gada soccer team used the stadium. They won the 1947 U.S. Open Cup and remained, at the end of the twentieth century, the last New England team to do so. In the 1950s and 1960s the area became a drive-in theater, and since the theater's closing, most of the site has remained empty.

ONE LAST CUP

In the spring of 1931, the Marksmen moved to New York and became the Yankees. However, because the team had started its National Open Cup quest that year playing as Fall River, the United States Soccer Federation recognized it by its original city and name throughout the tournament. Despite the fact that the New York Yankees won the trophy of 1931, the win is forever recorded as a victory for the Fall River Marksmen.

OPENED: 1922

CAPACITY: 5,000 seated

TENANT:

Shawsheen Indians (Industrial Soccer League); *soccer, 1923–1924*; (National Soccer League); *soccer, 1925*; (American Soccer League); *soccer, 1926*

Balmoral Park in Andover, Massachusetts, is unlike any other professional sports venue in Greater Boston. It had one of the shortest life spans as well as one of the longest; shortest in that it survived in the major leagues for only twenty-eight games back in 1926, but longest in that it survives today in much the same form as when it was created. The park was built for an amateur soccer team that shot up through the ranks at meteoric speed, reaching the pinnacle of the sport in this country, and then burned out just as fast. The park was sold and the stands removed, but to this day youth and adult amateur soccer is played there by both men and women.

SHAWSHEEN VILLAGE AND
THE AMERICAN WOOLEN COMPANY

The story of Balmoral Park begins in the first decade of the twentieth century and coincides with the history of William Madison Wood, president of the American Woolen Company. Wood, born of Armenian parents on Martha's Vineyard, Massachusetts, had begun his climb up the corporate ladder of the local textile giant. The firm was based on State Street in Boston, with the mill buildings located in Lawrence, twenty miles north of the city. As he gained control of American Woolen, he began implementing his dream of creating a model city to house executive offices and the people who would fill them. Shawsheen Village, as it was called, grew along the Shawsheen River in Andover, a small town of only eight thousand inhabitants, just south of Lawrence.

In 1906 he began amassing property for his project, and by 1918 he had obtained enough to start construction. Lying within the boundaries of the town of Andover, Shawsheen Village was nevertheless self-sufficient. His ideal town had every necessity. It contained a public garage for all automobiles; the Balmoral Spa, consisting of a drug store, restaurant, and ballroom; a post office across the street; and housing in two residential sections. Executives were to live in "Brick Shawsheen," on the west side of Main Street, while others would reside in "White Shawsheen" on the east. Also present were a bowling green and new corporate offices for the company.

(overleaf) FIGURE 53: The former Balmoral Park, home to the Shawsheen Indians of the American Soccer League, the 1925 National Open Cup champions. Soccer is still played there today, and it is now known as known as Shawsheen Field, 2004.

Courtesy of Dianne M. Foulds

SCOTSMAN WALLACE

Wood's private secretary, George M. Wallace, supervised the building of the village. His Scottish birth probably accounts for the street names in the village, such as York, Balmoral, and Argyle. Although William Wood was not a sports enthusiast, he consented to Wallace's plan to build a soccer field across from the executive headquarters. Bordered by Balmoral Street, York Street, and the Shawsheen River, and located in the center of the village, the park enjoyed an impressive setting.

FROM LOWLY BEGINNINGS

Toiling away in the amateur Industrial Soccer League at this time was an average amateur team run by a man named George Park. When Park stepped aside, the team asked Wallace—with a soccer background from his native Scotland—to step in. Wallace agreed and became totally involved. Using existing members as a base, he strengthened the team with higher-level players, all Scottish-born. The official name of the team was the Shawsheen Football Club, but it was known in community and league circles as the Indians.

To assure that the team had a home befitting its new status, his soccer field, Balmoral Park, was turned into a showplace, the envy of all opposing teams. Hand-laid sod was installed and a field house was built. The structure had locker rooms as well as hot showers, a feature none of the major league teams had yet obtained. Surrounding the playing surface was a quarter-mile track, and a grandstand holding five thousand seats.

STATE CHAMPIONS

The team entered the State Cup Tournament, open to all Massachusetts teams, both amateur and professional. Wallace's Shawsheen Indians had an easy time, and made it to the title game with relative ease.

May 10, 1924, saw a huge, partisan crowd fill Balmoral Park in Shawsheen Village for the championship finale against the Holyoke Falcos.

A STAR PLAYER

Arnie Oliver of New Bedford, left fullback for the Shawsheen Indians, continued his career after the Andover team folded. He returned home to New Bedford and played for the Clamdiggers of the American Soccer League. He was later elected to the National Soccer Hall of Fame, in Oneonta, New York.

Throughout the match, the Shawsheen eleven continually peppered their opponent's goal. For the first eighty minutes, however, they couldn't get the ball into the net. Dramatically, with only ten minutes remaining, McDermott beat the opposing goalie and the home team took the lead. With the bubble burst for Holyoke, it became easy for Shawsheen to score. Jock Corrigan, the star center forward, followed up only two minutes later, then put the icing on the cake five minutes after that. The final score: Shawsheen Indians, 3; Holyoke Falcos, 0.

State Association president Percy Wilson brought the cup to center field and presented it to team captain Charles Watson, declaring the Indians "best in Massachusetts." Watson, whose team had begun its rapid rise to the top, humbly reported he "was pleased to lead a state champion" (*Andover Townsman*, May 12, 1924). He also hoped that his opponents, the Falcos, who were such good sports, would win the title the next year.

MOVING ON UP

On August 16, team owner George M. Wallace invited all team players and hometown VIPs to a giant party at Brae Loch," an estate on Haggett's Pond. Following a feast, guests played in cricket matches, croquet tournaments, and even a pickup game of soccer. As the party wound down, George Wallace called everyone's attention for two announcements. He had been tracking his team's progress and felt it was time to "move up": he had accepted a franchise in the semiprofessional National League.

THE U.S. OPEN CUP

The U.S. Open Cup tournament is unique among American sporting events. Run by the United States Soccer Federation (USSF) since 1914, it is open to professional and amateur teams alike. No other major sport has a comparable arrangement. Imagine, if you will, the Boston Red Sox, Nashua Pride, and a local club team all vying for national honors in the same tournament.

According to the federation's rules, the only requirements for entry are that a team must belong to a league with at least four members, be affiliated with the USSF, and play a minimum of ten league matches a season. In recent years, the tournament has been dominated by members of Major League Soccer, but many well-known amateur teams have been successful throughout the cup tourney's history.

FORGE VILLAGE

Much like Shawsheen Village in Andover, Forge Village was created as a company town within the community of Westford, Massachusetts. The Abbot Worsted Company supported a soccer club and built a showplace field for the team's use, just as American Woolen had done in Andover. As the Forge Village and Shawsheen Village teams climbed the soccer ranks, their similarities and proximity made them natural rivals. On September 21, their first meeting ended in a tie. The two played again on November 9. That time Shawsheen eked out a 2–1 victory, clearing the path to a league title.

Despite its name, this new league was New England–based, but was considered among the best minor league circuits in the country. Secondly, he was considering entering the Indians in the prestigious U.S. Open Cup tournament. Admittedly, the task was daunting. Logic and history were against them: they would be up against the country's best teams, and no team had ever won the cup on its first try.

On Sunday, September 6, 1924, the team's debut in its new league came in Central Falls, Rhode Island, against the Waypoisett team. With the additions made to the roster, Wallace's group was strengthened somewhat. Six of the eleven starters from the previous year were gone. Tommy Murdoch was the new goalie and captain. Murdoch played superbly in goal, turning back almost every attack. Jack Kershaw, also new, had the honor of scoring the Indians' first National League goal, followed shortly by one from Tom McMasters. Shawsheen won its opener 2 to 1.

A week later the team came home to Balmoral Park to play Lorraine Mills in front of a thousand wildly cheering fans. The game proved an easy victory for Shawsheen as it racked up four goals while only allowing one. They immediately became favorites to win the league championship.

THE NATIONAL SCENE

Just before Christmas, Shawsheen clinched first place. Again, owner George Wallace made two announcements. He had secured a place in the American Soccer League, dominated by the nation's top teams, the best of which played just down the road in Boston. His second announcement was that Shawsheen would indeed be playing in the national tournament.

In January 1925, 128 teams lined up at the start, all vying for U.S. soccer supremacy. The Indians drew Arlington Mills in the first round, and fate was with Shawsheen from the start. Arlington Mills withdrew from the tournament, propelling the Indians automatically into round two.

In February, Shawsheen faced its first real challenge. The Indians played Boston on that team's home turf, the ancient Walpole Street Grounds. (For more information on the Boston Wonder Workers and the Walpole Street Grounds, also known as the South End Grounds, see chapter 1.) Boston was another relatively new team, but had established superiority early on by winning the famed Lewis Cup. That win had earned Boston the right to compete in the interleague championship against St. Louis, which it also won. In the 1925 Open Cup Tournament, however, victory belonged to Shawsheen.

Ironically, after the game the Boston team was honored at the White House by President Calvin Coolidge for its success at the interleague championship. Meanwhile, victorious Shawsheen moved into the next round of the National Open Cup Tournament.

On March 6 the Indians returned home to Balmoral Park to face the Whittal Team of Worcester; again Shawsheen triumphed. With the win, the team was now one of only eight left on the field. There was still a long way to go, but a national championship seemed more than an impossible dream.

Excitement mounted in Andover. The hometown team was now playing with the big boys. On March 27, the Indians traveled to Walpole Street in Boston to take on Bayonne, New Jersey. Again they came away with a win, this time by a score of 2–0.

The Shawsheen Indians had reached the semifinals; all of the Merrimack Valley took notice. Nearby Lawrence had always been a big soccer city. Through the years it had nurtured many good teams, but none had ever come close to what Shawsheen had done; in fact, only once before had a northern Massachusetts team reached the finals, and it had gone down to easy defeat to St. Louis. It was not only Shawsheen that was making headlines, though. Their chief nemesis from Forge Village, Abbot Worsted, had also made it this far. Regardless of the outcome, a Bay State team would therfore advance to the finals.

PLAYING FOR THE EASTERN TITLE

Boston Globe soccer editor, George M. Collins, reported, "Soccer fans from the Lawrence district had always dreamed of having a cup game. The one being played for the Eastern Title will be one of the greatest games ever staged, played for them at nearby Balmoral Park. Shawsheen Village and the contesting team will be two of their own pet aggregations." Another *Globe* writer declared, "[W]hile Shawsheen had a somewhat easy road to the semi-finals, nevertheless they are a sterling group of players, fit to compete with the best in the land" (*Boston Globe*, April 4, 1925).

To a man, every player proclaimed a readiness to battle for the chance to play in the grand finals against the western U.S. representative. Abbot had made it this far before only to be denied a trip to the finals—first by J & P Coats and later by Todd Shipyards. Abbot had no intention of being stopped by Shawsheen. The Indians answered by insisting that they would be the team advancing to soccer's blue-ribbon event. State Association president Wilson was elated that one of his teams would have a shot at the national title. "I expect Lawrence sports lovers to turn out as they have never turned out before."

Turn out they did. At 3 P.M. on Saturday, April 4, Balmoral Park was filled with spectators, owner George Wallace among them. He had had the field "prepared, primmed, and spruced up" so it would look the part it was now playing in soccer history.

Captain Ross won the coin toss and chose his end; Corrigan of Abbot kicked off. Electricity was in the air as Abbot Worsted pressed forward— in the first minute, Shawsheen's goalie, Tommy Murdoch, was forced to make two saves. A hand-ball call on a Shawsheen player made matters worse, giving Abbot a free kick near the goal, but Murdoch came through again. His great playing slowly turned the tide in the Indians' favor. Shawsheen now pressed forward. At the seventeen-minute mark, Alex Carrie, the Indians' center forward, got under a long punt down the field. He went up for the header and likely goal when he was grabbed at the ankle by an Abbot Worsted defender. The referee immediately signaled for a penalty kick. Shawsheen converted the penalty and put the

---

SHAWSHEEN TEAM IN THE 1925 CUP FINAL

Thomas Murdoch, goalie	Alexander Edwards, left wing
David Mills, left fullback	Edmund Smith, inside left
Bill Ross, right fullback	Alex Carrie, center forward
Fred Watkins, left halfback	Peter Purden, inside right
William Thomson, center halfback	Robert Blyth, right wing
Andrew Nixon, right halfback	

---

ball in the net for the first score of the day. Shawsheen controlled the play for most of the first half, but survived a close call when the ball flew over the crossbar, just as the halftime whistle blew.

When the second half began, Abbot Worsted attacked. They had to score or their season, and their dreams, would be over; they had to take chances with their defense. At midfield, Watkins made a perfect pass to center forward, Alex Carrie. Cosgrove of Abbot rushed in to stop him, but missed. A race toward the goal ensued. With Cosgrove beaten, the left fullback, Neal, tried to cover, but Carrie made a sharp, unexpected turn, and was all alone with only the goalie in the way. He drove the ball into the upper corner and Shawsheen was up by two. Carrie received handshakes from all his teammates as he headed back to the center of the field. It would prove to be the highlight of the match. Although defeat seemed imminent for them, Abbot Worsted played strong until the end. Just before the final whistle, Cummings, according to the *Andover Townsman*, "fastened onto a cross by Dundas" and Shawsheen was scored upon. No matter. The game ended and the home crowd went wild; the Shawsheen Indians were going to the finals.

ON TO THE U.S. OPEN CUP FINAL

With the Chicago Canadians victorious in the West, the final matchup was complete. George Collins of the *Globe* weighed in on the upcoming duel:

Massachusetts once more is represented in the final game for possession of the National Cup, emblematic of the soccer championship of the country. With all due respect to all other cups and championship tilts, Sunday's game at Tiverton is the classic. Will the Indians win the championship and rank with Fall River, Bethlehem Steel and Brooklyn, and all the other elevens who have won the famous trophy in years past?

April 19, 1775, was described by patriot Sam Adams as "a glorious morning for America." Weatherwise, April 19, 1925, was hardly that; the day began raw and overcast. In nearby Lexington and Concord, celebrations were underway marking 150 years since the American Revolution began. In Tiverton, more clouds had rolled in and the temperature continued to drop. Although all previous cup finals had seen crowds in the thousands, the 1925 matchup was seen by only "949 adults and 20 boys," according to the *Lawrence Eagle-Tribune*. Weather conditions kept what was expected to be an enormous turnout down to a minimum.

It didn't help that the home favorite, the Fall River Marksmen, had to sit in the stands and watch two outside squads battle for the title. They had been considered a potential winner when the tournament started. (For more information on the Fall River Marksmen, see chapter 13.)

Indians' fans were full of confidence but were wary of Chicago, a team described in the Boston papers as one of the best assembled machines ever to trot onto a soccer field. Players with major league experience filled its roster.

The cup game, billed as the "Grand Final," turned out to be a romp from start to finish. Shawsheen completely outclassed Chicago. One fan reported that Indians' goalie, Tommy Murdoch, was more or less a spectator.

Edmund Smith, inside left forward for Shawsheen, scored first, followed by a penalty kick scored by his line mate, inside right, Peter Purden. In the second half Alex Carrie made it 3–0. At that point, Shawsheen pulled back and defended its lead. The Indians looked strong enough to double their score but seemed satisfied with what they had.

The Shawsheen Indians, champions of the nation, brought the title home to Andover. They were a team that had started in a local amateur league and then had climbed to the top in four years. Teams owned by all of the great factories of the East Coast had fallen by the wayside, and George M. Wallace hoisted the cup for his little town team.

BURNOUT

The future seemed bright for the Shawsheen eleven. They were now sitting atop soccer's highest peak, with an invitation to join the American Soccer League, the nation's best.

The brilliance lasted only as long as a Fourth of July sparkler, though. The Shawsheen Indians never again enjoyed the success and fame they had that year. They did enter the American Soccer League for the 1925–26 season and got to play the likes of the Boston Wonder Workers, Providence Clam Diggers, Indiana Flooring, Brooklyn, and Philadelphia, but the franchise only lasted for twenty-eight games, or about half of the schedule. On March 27, 1926, they played their last match, losing to Boston.

They had started the season well, winning ten of the first fifteen, but fell into a tailspin, losing ten of the next thirteen. In early April, George Wallace closed down operations and moved to California. He stated the reason as "lack of patronage." However, the demise of the Shawsheen Indians may have had more to do with outside influences than

FIGURE 54: George M. Wallace, owner of the Shawsheen Indians, with the 1925 National Soccer Championship banner. *Courtesy Eagle-Tribune Publishing Company*

small crowds. Just a month earlier, company president William Madison Wood, Wallace's employer and patron of the team, committed suicide, in part because American Woolen's fortunes had taken a turn for the worse. New president Andrew Pierce immediately began selling corporate property. The move to Shawsheen had never been popular with company executives, so the decision was made to put the headquarters back in Boston's financial district. The soccer field was the first property to go. The little local team that shot out of nowhere—taking its fans on one fantastic, wild ride—was no more. That, however, in no way diminishes the fact that for one magical spring, the Shawsheen Indians of Andover, Massachusetts, made it to the big leagues.

Although the team and the American Woolen Company were gone from the village, Balmoral Park lived on. For many years it served as the athletic fields for the Sacred Heart School, which had moved into the vacated corporate headquarters of the woolen company. Today called Shawsheen Field, it is owned by the town of Andover. Although the grandstand is long gone, the park still sports soccer goalposts, for the game that the park was built for is very much alive at the old field.

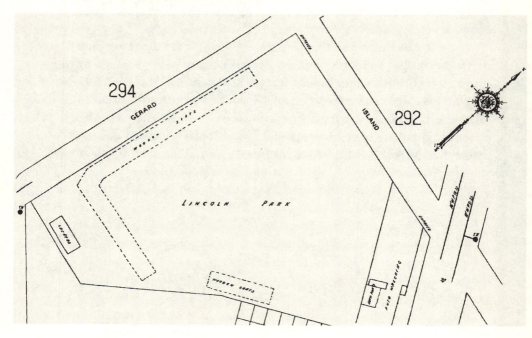

OPENED: Approximately 1930

CLOSED: approximately 1936

FIELD MEASUREMENTS: Left field 300 feet (approximately)
   Deep center field 400 feet (approximately)
   Right field 180 feet (approximately)

CAPACITY: 6,000

TENANTS:

Boston Tigers; *baseball, 1930 to 1936*
Philly Giants; *baseball, 1930 to 1936*
Boston Giants; *baseball, 1932*
Boston Royal Giants; *baseball, 1934–1936*
Boston Pullman Porters; *baseball, 1934*
Colored House of David; *baseball, 1934*
Boston ABCs; *baseball, 1935*

Lincoln Park is Boston's forgotten field. It is a nearly invisible part of the city's past. No photographs appear to be available, yet it played an important role in Boston's African-American sports history for the decade of the 1930s. During that period no less than seven minor league teams called Lincoln Park their home.

From the late 1800s to 1947 a so-called gentleman's agreement between baseball's major league owners kept a sizable portion of the population from playing "America's game." Some of the best players ever to step to the plate or throw from the mound were denied the chance to do so in the major leagues for no other reason than the color of their skin. Although the agreement was never put into writing, and its existence was even denied by those in power, it was strictly enforced. One wonders what early organized baseball would have been like with such stars as Satchel Paige, Josh Gibson, "Buck" Leonard, Monte Irvin, and "Cool Papa" Bell playing in their prime.

This, of course, is not news. Many stories have been told of Jackie Robinson's bravery and Branch Rickey's statesmanship in changing the course of sports history. These men did not erase the evils of the past, but their actions ensured that future generations of baseball players would no longer be subjected to the indignity of automatic exclusion. The day that the Brooklyn Dodgers broke the color barrier, according to the *Boston Chronicle*, a newspaper that catered primarily to Boston's predominantly black neighborhoods, "was the day baseball truly became the *national* pastime."

THE NEGRO LEAGUES

With the gates to the National and American Leagues closed to those of African descent, a parallel universe developed. Black leagues formed, offering professional careers to those with baseball ability. An early attempt included a team from Boston, but the club never played a home game. Formed in February 1887, the National Colored Base Ball League listed the Boston Resolutes as charter members. Other teams were located in Louisville, Baltimore, Philadelphia, Pittsburgh, and New

(opposite) FIGURE 55: Insurance map from the 1930s showing the location of Lincoln Park in an area once known as the Roxbury Wharf District. The field was located in a block surrounded by Island Street, Gerard Street, and Chesterton Street. *Copyright 1914, 1943, The Sanborn Map Company, The Sanborn Library, LLC. All rights Reserved. Further reproductions prohibited without written permission from The Sanborn Library, LLC.*

York. According to baseball historian John Holway, Boston won its first scheduled game in Louisville, playing the Falls City club. Unfortunately it was the only game played before the collapse of the fledgling organization. The league went out of business, Holway explained, and the players had to find jobs as waiters to earn enough to make it back to Boston.

The first Negro National League was formed in 1920 by noted promoter Rube Foster, and was probably the most successful of the African-American leagues. A second National League came to life on the death of the first, and continued in operation until 1949.

Other leagues, such as the American Negro League, Eastern Colored League, and East-West League, sprang up as well. Such teams as the Kansas City Monarchs, Homestead Grays, Pittsburgh Crawfords, New York Colored Giants, and Brooklyn Elite Giants made names for themselves as large as any of the teams in the all-white majors. Their all-star games, played at Commisky Park in Chicago, drew from all parts of the population, filling the stands.

THE BOSTON BLACK TEAMS

The city of Boston played only a peripheral role in the formation and continuation of the various black major leagues. For close to fifty years, attempts were made by the locals to create one true team for the area to support. Instead, the city saw a parade of clubs form, disappear, and sometimes reappear, but never quite capture the entire city's imagination.

There are several reasons for their lack of success. There was competition from the Braves and Red Sox; there was a high degree of racism; and, additionally, the talent was spread too thin among so many teams. No one club ever managed to break away from the pack.

In Boston a few dedicated promoters, players, and journalists kept the flame alive in Lincoln Park, a stadium that the community could call its own, as well as at available public parks.

In 1903 the first Boston Royal Giants came to life, joining the Greater Boston League. They played against such rivals as the Medford Independents, Cambridge Washingtons, Malden Riversides, West Newton, and Allston. This was the first version of a team that would exist off and on in one form or another for half a century.

Some time before the First World War, the Royal Giants were supplanted as the local favorites by the Boston Tigers, managed by Bob Russell. Russell would be involved with the black baseball community beyond just the management of his team; he promoted local games with

CARTER PLAYGROUND

Originally known as the Columbus Avenue Playground, the park was renamed for Sergeant William E. Carter on July 20, 1920. During the last days of the South End Grounds the two parks stood side by side, with the Carter field sitting just to the northeast of the other, on Columbus Avenue. The park was used by black teams, both amateur and semi-pro, until 1949. Complete with its original concrete bleachers, it stands today, still hosting local amateur baseball.

many of the big teams from around the country. During the 1920s, management of the Tigers was taken over by promoter, Arthur A. Johnson, who ran the team until 1935.

These early teams had no home of their own, but played their games at local public parks such as the Dorchester Town Field and the more popular Carter Playground. At the public parks, no formal admission was charged. Rather, a hat was passed and donations were made to support the team. There was an advantage to this arrangement. Since the teams were officially amateur clubs, games could be played on Sundays; a right not granted to the Braves or Red Sox until 1928.

LINCOLN PARK

After the First World War, land on Massachusetts Avenue, formerly occupied by a Boston Consolidated Gas tank, was turned into a private baseball diamond. The Boston Tigers were the first to move in, followed closely by the Philadelphia Colored Giants, a Boston semi-pro club. The Philadelphia Colored Giants were not a Pennsylvania team; many of the players, however, originally came from Philadelphia. Local fans shortened the name to Philly Giants.

Unlike the playgrounds in Dorchester or on Columbus Avenue, Lincoln Park was enclosed and included a ticket booth and locker rooms. The longer part of the wooden grandstand ran parallel to the third-base line, along Gerard Street in Roxbury. The first-base stand attached to the third-base seats behind home plate and ran perpendicular from them, along Chesterton Street. A separate set of bleachers also ran parallel to Chesterton, further into the outfield. The locker room sat just outside the grandstand, at the edge of the fence, near the corner of Chesterton and Gerard Streets. The stadium took up most of the block surrounded by Gerard, Chesterton, and Island Streets, and Massachusetts Avenue, near its junction with Southampton Street.

Industrial structures filled the immediate neighborhood surrounding the park. In the 1930s, two holding tanks and a storage building, owned by the Boston Consolidated Gas Company, stood within sight of home plate. Known at one time as Roxbury Central Wharf, and later as South Bay, the neighborhood around Lincoln Park is, to this day, a commercial district.

In 1931, due to the efforts of Arthur "Daddy" Black, the Providence Colored Giants were born. The team was based in Rhode Island, but scheduled several games at Lincoln Park. Mr. Black created the Giants as a fully professional organization. The successful black teams of the past, such as Dan Whitehead's Providence group, had worked under a co-pay system, whereby active players divided a certain percentage of the gate among themselves. Arthur Black, on the other hand, offered guaranteed salaries to his players, ranging from forty dollars to sixty dollars a week.

His team did not rely on public parks, with open admission. In Boston with the Giants, he chose to play at Lincoln Park because it was enclosed and tickets could be sold.

Daddy Black was murdered during a holdup in Providence on September 14, 1932, when five men broke into his Cranston Street office. Having endured heavy financial losses, as well as the death of its owner, the Colored Giants did not survive.

The "Rover" column in the *Boston Chronicle* offered its own point of view: "The venture was a complete failure. [The problem] can be traced primarily to prima donnas carried by the team. The late owner made the fatal mistake of paying these hired help weekly salaries" (April 1, 1933). The newspaper felt strongly that the co-pay methods employed by the older Black Providence teams were superior.

THE LINCOLN PARK ERA

The 1930s represented a golden era for black baseball in Boston. Although no one team managed to dominate, or even to offer continuity, there were always clubs ready to fill any gaps that occurred. To be considered the community's prime club, a team had to make Lincoln Park its home. As the *Boston Chronicle* commented, "Any club establishing its teepee at Lincoln Park automatically becomes the bigshot hereabouts." Although the parks were not comparable in size, the newspaper on several occasions made reference to Lincoln in the same light

as Fenway Park and Braves Field.

In 1932 the Boston Tigers of the New England League were still the main attraction at the stadium, and were often called the "Lincoln Park Nine." Also still playing at the "Southampton ground," as the *Chronicle* often called the park, were the Philly Giants. The two clubs were joined by the Boston Colored Giants, managed by former Negro League star Oliver Marcelle. A traditional "old-timers" game, played each summer, had formerly been staged at Carter Playground; along with the new team, this annual classic also moved into Lincoln Park. Admission for most games was fifteen cents.

Promoter Billy Leonard brought excitement to the park in 1933. He arranged for the Brooklyn Cuban Giants to travel north to take on the Philly Giants. On two separate days the teams squared off three times, with wide-ranging results. Several thousand spectators filled the stands first in a slight rain and then under a torrid sun. In the first matchup the visitors romped, beating the locals 16–1. In the double-header a week later, another full house witnessed the Giants turn it around, winning the first game 18–2, and the second by a score of 11–9. The *Chronicle* stated, "It was a slugfest that exceeds all past baseball exhibitions ever staged at the Southampton Street bandbox" (*Boston Chronicle*, September 9, 1933).

Babe Ruth had promised to throw out the first ceremonial ball at a game in Lincoln Park in June 1934, but his own game at Fenway Park went into extra innings, preventing his visit.

Several additional clubs emerged in 1934 in Boston. The Pullman Porters moved into Lincoln Park. James Green, organizer of the team, also took over management of the park for the year. A group calling itself the "Colored House of David" took up residence there as well. This team had no connection to the famous House of David barnstormers from

THE GIANTS

Black teams in Boston and elsewhere sported similar names. Many included the word "Giants" in their moniker. Very popular were Royal Giants, Elite Giants, Bachrach Giants, and so forth. According to Buck O'Neil, famed Negro League player and author, the inclusion of the word "Giants" was code to mean a black team. Many newspapers at the time would not print photographs of African-Americans. When one saw a poster announcing that the Royal Giants or Elite Giants were coming, the baseball fan, black or white, knew that the team was probably a black club.

Bent Harbor, Michigan. That club from the Midwest, sporting signature long beards, had become so well-known that baseball organizations from around the country began imitating them. The Hub club was just another example of this.

The year also welcomed a new version of the Boston Royal Giants, under the direction of Burlin White, a fixture in the local baseball scene for twenty years, who served as both manager and catcher for the club. The Royal Giants played their games at Lincoln Park as well as Carter Playground.

As 1935 arrived, the lineup of teams was similar to the year before. Gone, however, was the House of Davids, replaced by the Boston ABCs. Manager Clem Mack leased Lincoln Park for the year and his club became its prime tenant. In the off-season he had a new pavilion built, as part of a refurbishing project at the grounds. On Sunday, June 2, opening-day ceremonies for the rejuvenated park included a double-header between his ABCs and the Gold Seal Shoe club of Lynn.

Clem Mack added to the park's revenue stream by leasing the facility to other sports groups. In 1935 Lincoln Park hosted portions of the state soccer tournament, as well as black semiprofessional football.

Although the Pullman Porters had disbanded by 1935, the Philly Giants were back, as were the Boston Tigers and Burlin White's Royal Giants. White's contingent started the season playing in Canada. Overall his team racked up its best record, finishing with eighty-seven wins, compared with twenty-two losses and five ties. At one point the Royals were victorious in thirty-one straight games.

A ROYAL GIANTS UNIFORM

In 1942 Herbert "Chink" Holmes was a pitcher and shortstop for the Boston Royal Giants. Although little is recorded of his baseball career, his uniform, emblazoned with "Boston" across the chest, the logo "RG" on the left shoulder, and Holmes' number 2 on the back, lives on. Following his death in 1995 the uniform was discovered among his belongings and his grandson, Tracy McDaniel of Bos-

ton, loaned it to the Negro Leagues Baseball Museum in Kansas City.

On July 13, 2002, in a game between the Boston Red Sox and the Toronto Blue Jays at the Skydome, black baseball was honored. Each team took the field in the uniform of a Negro League club. The Red Sox chose to represent the Boston Royal Giants, and played the game in uniforms modeled after the one worn by Chink Holmes.

BEGINNING OF THE END

By 1936 a movement was underway to bring some organization to the local black baseball scene. Arthur Johnson of the Tigers called for a March meeting to discuss the idea of a Boston league. According to the *Boston Chronicle*, since the meeting produced no results, Burlin White of the Royal Giants called for a "Grand Baseball Fest at Lincoln Park on May 17th and 18th" (April 25, 1936). The contest would include his own team, as well as the Philly Giants and the Providence team. This game, too, did not take place.

As the dust settled, only the Philly Giants and Royal Giants appear to have survived the year, but Lincoln Park, central to the black teams in Boston, appears never to have hosted another game. The surviving teams moved back to the public parks, and big games were scheduled elsewhere. On June 16, 1940, the Homestead Grays of Pittsburgh played the Fraser All-Stars under the lights in Lynn. In September 1942 Fenway Park played host to the Philadelphia Stars and Baltimore Elite Giants. Promoter Bob Russell brought the New York Cuban Giants to Fenway as well, but poor publicity brought out only a thousand fans.

Also in 1942 a circuit called the New Negro Baseball League planned to include the Boston Royal Giants, who would play alongside the Chicago Brown Bombers, Cincinnati Clowns, Baltimore Black Eagles, Minneapolis–St. Paul Gophers, and Detroit Red Sox. Instead the Giants played out their days in Boston's Park League.

PART THREE

THEY ALSO PLAYED A ROLE

Mechanics Building, Boston, Mass.

FIGURE 56: A postcard view of the Massachusetts Charitable Mechanic Association block at 99-111 Huntington Avenue, ca. 1920. This view of the Mechanics Building looks up Huntington Avenue toward West Newton Street. It was the temporary home of the Boston Trojans of the American Basketball Association. *Courtesy of Bostonian Society/Old State House; creator, M. Abrams, Roxbury, MA*

Not every sports team has had the luxury of building its own venue, or even of having one readily available. Some organizations struggled through the early years in whatever arena or field that was available at the time, only years later securing an acceptable facility. Many never made it past the formative years. Still others started big, only to end their days at a less than satisfactory, but affordable, home. Because many of the teams were not in a financial position to be discriminating, they often found homes several miles outside of Boston. Inner suburbs, such as Cambridge, Revere, Lynn, and Malden, hosted teams, as did communities as far as twenty miles to the north (North Andover), and west (Framingham).

Through its sports history Boston has been labeled a "baseball town." Other sports can have their day, but it is always baseball that the fan returns to. Proof of this lies in the fact that each of the city's major league baseball teams—whether they lasted one year, eighty-one years, or one hundred and one years and counting—has always managed to build its own park, each touted at the time as the best such facility in the nation. (Hockey has been nearly as fortunate: although the Bruins did not build the Arena or Garden, those sites were considered more-than-acceptable major league arenas in their eras.)

Other sports, such as basketball and football until 1971, however, have been left to fend for themselves, usually with little or no money. Those teams negotiated for available time at high-school and college stadiums, function halls, and parks in order to pursue their major league dreams.

What follows is the story of the parks and arenas that have hosted professional sports teams, which by circumstance or design never made it to the big leagues. Some were meant to be temporary facilities. Some turned out to be "starter homes" for teams that eventually blossomed. In a few cases the stadiums hosted only a single big event; others were built for minor league teams. In all cases, though, they played a part in Boston-area sports history.

FIGURE 57: Harvard Stadium; ca. 1920. The stadium is home to Harvard's football team. It also served as temporary home to the Boston Patriots before their stadium was built in Foxborough, Mass. In 1984 a small portion of the Summer Olympics was held here, complete with Olympic flame and cauldron. *Courtesy of Boston Public Library, Print Department*

HARVARD STADIUM

PROFESSIONAL TENANTS:
Boston Patriots (National Football League); *football, 1970*
Soccer Games of the XXIII Los Angeles Olympiad
CAPACITY: 30,898

Although well-known far and wide in its role as the nation's oldest college sports facility, Harvard Stadium has also played host to many major events throughout its long and storied existence. In addition to being the site for several hundred Crimson football games, it has welcomed rugby matches, track meets, a few hockey games, and even concerts by well-known artists. It hosted football's Boston Patriots for a season, while that team's permanent home in Foxborough was being constructed, and when the venerable structure was eighty-one years old, it even served briefly as an Olympic site. Built in 1903, it stands today as Boston's, and probably the nation's, oldest existing structure once used for professional sports.

Harvard Stadium, known simply as "the Stadium" in Cambridge, has sat on its Charles River perch on the Boston side of the river since long before there was a National Football League, National Hockey League, or National Basketball Association. Before it was built, Harvard's football squad played at a number of sites, including Jarvis Field and Holmes Field on campus, as well as the South End Baseball Grounds in Boston. To create a permanent home for its team, the class of 1879 donated the Stadium as its twenty-fifth anniversary gift. Before construction could begin, however, the college had to be convinced of the feasibility of the project. Some thought that a concrete structure of that size could not survive many harsh New England winters. Eventually, with most nay-sayers convinced that the plan was sound, the project got underway. At a cost of $310,000, and a time line of four and a half months, Harvard Stadium became a reality and an instant landmark.

It opened one month after the first World Series ended at nearby Huntington Avenue and it was considered an engineering masterpiece, marking the first time a massive, reinforced-concrete structure was built for American college athletics. Unlike in previous football fields, the seating was placed very close to the edge of the playing surface.

Throughout the twentieth century the Stadium was the site of many well-known collegiate matchups, including several editions of the famous Harvard-Yale rivalry. That annual classic against Harvard's counterparts from New Haven is called simply, The Game.

A CHANGE IN THE RULES

According to Harvard's Sports Media Relations department, the proximity of the seating to the playing surface at Harvard Stadium had a direct impact on the future of American football.

In 1906 there was much discussion about the sport's roughness.... When the football rules com-mittee met to propose changes, its secretary, Yale's Walter Camp, pushed the idea of widening the field by as much as 40 feet to open up the game. However, the idea could not be implemented without considerable alterations to the Stadium. Instead, the forward pass was adopted.

HARVARD WINS 29–29

On November 23, 1968, the most talked-about edition of the traditional football matchup between Harvard and Yale took place. Each team went into the league finale with a perfect 8–0 record. The Ivy League title was on the line. With only forty-two seconds remaining, Harvard trailed Yale's Bulldogs by a score of 29–13. Miraculously, the boys from Cambridge came up with sixteen points in less than a minute, tying the score. The game and season ended in a dead heat. The next day's headline of the *Harvard Crimson* read, "Harvard Wins 29–29." No one argued.

Harvard Stadium's "professional career" began in August 1960, in a game kicking off the first American Football League season. In an exhibition match, the Dallas Texans defeated the Boston Patriots. The new sports entity in town drew eleven thousand fans.

In 1970 the Patriots—whose regular home field that year was at Boston University—returned to Harvard Stadium. In its final year as the Boston Patriots, the team played its entire season at the Stadium. The next year, they moved into the brand-new Schaeffer Stadium in Foxborough and renamed themselves the New England Patriots. (For more information on Foxboro Stadium, see chapter 8.)

In 1984 Harvard Stadium added further luster to its already bright history when it was chosen as the site of several Olympic events. Although the bulk of the Olympic Games were being held in the city of Los Angeles, the organizers of the games spread some of the events across the country: Terre Haute, Pasadena, Palo Alto, and Annapolis were designated as satellite sites, as was Boston. For the first time, soccer was played at the Stadium as the Olympic teams of Cameroon, Canada, Chile, France, Iraq, Norway, and Qatar saw action here. The games at Harvard Stadium began with opening ceremonies, complete with an Olympic flame, skydivers, and the release of hundreds of balloons. On Sunday, July 29, 1984, Vice President George H. W. Bush was on hand at Harvard Stadium to take part in the lighting of the local Olympic Cauldron.

On September 6, 1986, the grand finale of the school's 350th Anniversary celebration took place at Harvard Stadium. The show featured the world-renowned Boston Pops, a laser show, and Walter Cronkite of CBS News as host.

REVERE BEACH BICYCLE TRACKS

Professional bicycle racing was a staple at Revere Beach for much of the first half of the twentieth century. The beach, once called the "Playground of New England," was a major amusement area, featuring roller coasters, nightclubs, touring acts, and a variety of other entertainment. The Revere Cycle Track, the first of three stadiums built in Revere for bicycle racing, was built in 1901 by A. A. McLean on Ocean Avenue. After operating the track for twelve years, he sold out to famed cyclist Nat Butler in 1913.

Butler, a resident of the Point of Pines section of the city, built the business up; crowds as large as eight thousand for major events were not uncommon. Butler was a showman and knew how to attract an audience. On April 19 (Patriot's Day), 1917, he opened the season with a parade of bikes around the one-eighth-mile track, and followed that with a band concert. He invited Governor McCall and the mayor of Revere as guests of honor. (Their special box seat was adorned with a flag that had been presented to Butler by the president of France when Butler won the world championship.) The event cost twenty-five cents.

Business was apparently so good that Butler tore down the first Revere Cycle Track in 1919 and replaced it with a newer version on North Shore Road, in what is today the parking lot for the Wonderland Dog Track. A decade later business declined, and in 1929 Butler introduced boxing matches to shore up gate receipts. This new venture was scheduled for Thursday nights with admissions ranging from fifty cents to a dollar-fifty. Boxing was not enough to save the track, however. On November 16, 1931, a wrecking crew began razing the structure.

Butler stayed in the bicycle-racing field, sponsoring six-day events at Boston Garden, while he built a third and final track, the Revere Velodrome Bicycle Track, in the Beachmont section of Revere. Just four years later the site became part of the Suffolk Downs Horse Race track.

NAT BUTLER

Nat Butler was born in Halifax, Nova Scotia, of Irish parents. During his early career he was a champion rider, known by hundreds of thousands of sports fans in both the United States and Europe. A highlight was his 1909 victory in the Golden Wheel Championship in Cologne, Germany. In 1913 there was a race in France named in his honor, "Le Prix Nat Butler."

"RACING ETIQUETTE"

Former bicycle racer Jimmy Brown tells the story of his initiation into racing at Revere. He had started his career in Scotland. Upon arriving in the Boston area, in the 1920s he signed up for a multilap race, in which the leader at the end of each lap would receive a dollar. A grand prize went to the overall winner. In similar races at the track, he had noticed that there was a different leader after each lap, but when he entered he led for the entire race. This earned him all lap prizes as well as the grand prize. He repeated the feat in a few more contests, much to the chagrin of the other riders. In his fifth race, while at the top of the banked, wooden track, one of his competitors pushed an object into his wheel, causing him to slide down the track toward the middle of the velodrome, picking up hundreds of splinters along the way. Realizing his breach of etiquette, he never raced there again, opting instead to remain a spectator. In all future races, the prize money was once again evenly divided among participants.

MALDEN STADIUM

The Pearl Street park in Malden, Massachusetts, today known as Mac-Donald Stadium, was the scene of a Patriot's Day showdown in 1927 between Boston's professional soccer team and one of the powers of the world. The Boston Wonder Workers, who normally played their league matches at the South End Grounds in Boston, traveled north to Malden on that April 19 to meet Uruguay, the Olympic champs. (For more information on the South End Grounds and the Boston Wonder Workers, see chapter 1.) By contemporary accounts, Boston bested them in both the game and the ensuing riot.

The match was billed as a showdown between top teams of each American continent. Uruguay had won the gold medal at the Paris Olympic Games of 1924, and would, three years later, take home the first Fédération Internationale de Football Association (FIFA) World Cup. Nine starters from the tournament at the Olympics were on hand to play in Malden, including Mazzall, who had built a reputation as one of the world's premier goalies. The Boston Wonder Workers had won the National Professional Championship two years earlier and would go on to win the American League trophy later that season.

The South American team members were treated as visiting dignitaries. On the day before the holiday they were welcomed at the State House 189 in Boston by Governor Alvan Fuller. They retired early in order to stay sharp for the game and keep the record of their American tour clean.

When the Uruguayans arrived at the stadium Governor Fuller, a resident of Malden, was once again the host. Despite the heat and humidity, more than six thousand soccer fans showed up to cheer the home team and to marvel at the talented visitors.

The first half saw great action and an even game as both teams scored a goal, but things got rough later in the match as Boston took a 3–2 lead. What happened next is open to debate. According to the *Boston Globe*, "[T]he temperaments of the Olympic champs became pronounced as the game progressed. The climax came when Cea [of Uruguay] deliberately kicked McIntyre and then tried to slam the Boston captain. Priestly went to help and Petrone kicked him" (April 20, 1927). The *Malden Evening News* presented a different slant, reporting that some "spectators saw Bobby Blair of Boston swing on Castro of the Olympic team" (April 20, 1927). In a third version, also reported by the *News*, game organizer William Kennedy reported: "The trouble started when Jack McArthur of the Boston team was swung on by Scaroni, the Inside Right for Uruguay" (April 20, 1927).

In any event, a melee ensued. Players from both teams were fighting and approximately two thousand fans from the grandstand joined the fray. The Malden police closed in to restore order, and the referee called a temporary halt to the game until tempers cooled. When the dust settled two Boston players, Ernest Priestly of Lexington and Thomas McMillan of Winthrop, were unconscious. All of the Uruguay team "left under their own power, but carried away a variety of 'souvenirs' which they will be nursing for many days," according to the *News*. They refused to come back on the field when called, so the game was ended and victory awarded to Boston.

The Uruguayans boarded their team bus and left the city under a police escort.

GE FIELD

Although never a major league ballpark, GE Field in Lynn, Massachusetts, nonetheless deserves a footnote in the annals of baseball history. On Friday, June 24, 1927, the lights switched on, a game was played at night, and sports would never be the same.

GE Field, operated by the General Electric Employee Athletic Association, was not the first park illuminated for evening games. Night games are recorded as far back as September 2, 1880, when the Jordan Marsh team played R. H. White, in a battle of the department stores on Nantasket Beach in Hull, Massachusetts. Both football and soccer had experimented with lights in the past. The role GE Field played that night was one of a prototype for the major leagues. Engineers from the General Electric Company had designed the lighting, and representatives from both the American and National Leagues were on hand to witness an amateur game scheduled between a Lynn and a Salem club.

Originally scheduled for June 23, the game was scrubbed because of rain. Although the storm had abated, the field was slick and the organizers wanted nothing to interfere with their experiment in night baseball. They used the extra day for fine-tuning and testing. Game or no game, nearly two thousand curious spectators arrived at the park on the twenty-third just to see the lights turned on. Several major league and college representatives spent the evening examining the field from all angles, under the lights. President Quinn of the Red Sox walked the base paths with Father Mattimore, athletic director for Boston College, taking notes and making observations. At second base, Quinn commented, "We can see grounders here all right, and we haven't played baseball for several years." Following the tour, representatives from the Boston and Washington clubs fired questions at the engineers. Quinn suggested using searchlights rather than floodlights for illumination of the upper air, cutting down on glare. Acting on the Red Sox suggestion, GE installed four large searchlights before the game.

The next night, on a dry field, the resceduled game took place. When the lights first came on, the players seemed to shy away from the plate for fear of being hit by a pitch they might not see coming; this tendency dissipated as the game wore on. Initially there had been fear of an error-prone game, but this also did not seem to be a problem. Lynn was victorious over Salem 7–2, with only two errors recorded.

By all accounts the game was a huge success. Bucky Harris of Washington was most enthusiastic, and Bill Carrigan of the Red Sox had nothing but praise for the engineers. Goose Gosselin of Washington said that he would now be willing to play night games under the conditions he had witnessed, but preferred even more lighting. Before the night was out, General Electric authorities received a telegram from the Jersey City Baseball Club requesting that the company illuminate its stadium for night play in the International League.

New England League head Claude Davidson predicted that night   191 games would be a regular feature in the majors before the decade was out. His prediction was not far off the mark: the first night game in the major leagues occurred eight years later. On the evening of May 24, 1935, Crosley Field in Cincinnati lit up, under the direction of GE engineers. By 1946 lights came on in Boston at Braves Field, and a year later at Fenway.

EVERETT STADIUM

PROFESSIONAL TENANTS: Boston Wonder Workers
(American Soccer League); *soccer, 1929*
Boston Celtics (American Soccer League); *soccer, 1931–1932*

Everett Stadium, on the Revere Beach Parkway in Everett, Massachusetts, is the home ground of that city's high-school sports teams. It has also been the site of many professional soccer games. In February 1929 the ancient South End Grounds, home to the Boston Wonder

---

EARLY PROFESSIONAL BASKETBALL

Before the Boston Celtics began play in the National Basketball Association, the city had seen two attempts at the professional sport come and go. The Boston Whirlwinds lived up to their name, blowing into town and disappearing before the year was out. After a six-week stint at the Boston Arena, they played for two weeks at the Mechanics Building on the corner of West Newton Street and Huntington Avenue. That Gothic style, four-story building has since been replaced by the Prudential Center and the Hynes Convention Center. The Whirlwinds' final stop was on Highland Avenue in Somerville, at the Mount Benedict Knights of Columbus Hall.

The Knights of Columbus have long since moved but the structure stands today, serving as a private function hall.

A decade after the demise of the Whirlwinds a second team made a similar attempt, and suffered a similar fate. The Boston Trojans began life at Boston Arena but within three months had moved to the Irvington Street Armory, playing in the National Guard Drill Hall. Also known as the "South Armory," it was situated along the western edge of the New York, New Haven, and Hartford Railroad tracks, running lengthwise from Dartmouth Street to Irvington Street, across from the Harcourt Building. It was built in what had been the outfield of the Dartmouth Street Baseball Grounds, and is today the site of the Copley Place shopping mall. (For more information on the Dartmouth Street Grounds, see chapter 10.)

Workers of the American Soccer League, were closed down. (For more information on the South End Grounds, see chapter 1.) For the remainder of the season, therefore, the Wonder Workers plied their trade in Everett. A later soccer team, the Celtics, moved into Everett Stadium in the early 1930s. Once again, in May 1964, the field saw soccer action as the Boston Metros of a new American League hosted the Liverpool Football Club of the English League. Liverpool beat the locals 8–1.

LYNN'S STADIUMS

Sitting next to each other, Manning Bowl and Fraser Field in Lynn, Massachusetts, were both built for school sports during the Depression, and both have housed professional sports. Each is distinctive in appearance, having been constructed for a particular sport, but they share a common legacy.

Manning Bowl

PROFESSIONAL TENANT:
Boston Shamrock Rovers (United Soccer Association); *soccer, 1967*

Manning Bowl, the older of the two parks, opened on Thanksgiving Day in 1937 to a packed house of 10,200 partisans. Loyalties were divided equally between the city's high schools, "Classical" and "English," in the traditional holiday football showdown. No special ceremonies marked the occasion, but architect Cyril Harding was on hand to make sure that all details were worked out satisfactorily.

In 1967 the stadium was used as part of an experiment unique to American professional sports. The brand-new United Soccer Association (USA) formed, with hopes of becoming America's newest major league. The circuit originally planned on debuting the following year, but competition from a rival group with the same idea forced the organization to start early. The National Professional Soccer League, also with aspirations to major league status, planned an earlier start. None of the teams of the USA had been built yet, so each franchise owner invited a team from Europe or South America. Both continents were inactive during the summer months, making it easy for teams to relocate temporarily. The Boston organization, owned by the Adams family of Boston Bruins fame, hired the Shamrock Rovers of Dublin. The Rovers, well-known in their native country, have played at Milltown Road in Dublin since 1901, and have won the championship of the

League of Ireland more than a dozen times. Their stars, such as Liam Tuohy and Paddy Mulligan, were household names throughout Ireland in the 1960s.

For the 1967 summer season, the Boston Shamrock Rovers played at Manning Bowl, battling other Old World clubs such as Stoke City of England, playing as Cleveland, and Glentoran, their rivals from the north, representing Detroit for the year.

By 1968 the United Soccer Association and its competitors from the National Professional Soccer League had merged to become the North American League. Boston's franchise from the National circuit won out, and the Shamrock Rovers returned to Ireland. Today they are still one of the best-known clubs in that nation.

Fraser Field

PROFESSIONAL TENANTS:

Lynn Red Sox; *baseball, 1940s*
Lynn Sailors/Pirates (Eastern Baseball League); *baseball, 1980–1982*
Massachusetts Mad Dogs (North Atlantic Baseball League);
baseball, 1990s
North Shore Spirit (Northeast Baseball League); *baseball, 2003–present*

Manning Bowl's counterpart for baseball is Fraser Field. The park, named for Lynn baseball patron Eugene Fraser, opened to much fanfare on June 18, 1940. Following a parade through town and dedication ceremonies at the park, the local amateur Fraser Club of the Suburban Twilight League played the Pittsburgh Pirates, under the management of Frankie Frisch. Bob Quinn, president of the Boston Braves, was in attendance, as were the mayors and selectmen of most nearby towns.

Like its football counterpart next door, Fraser Field's main tenants were the city's high-school teams, but it has seen its share of professional games throughout its history. Not long after opening day, the Fraser Club again took on a major league team. On July 16th a famous black team, the Homestead Grays, came to Lynn and defeated the home side, 10–3, under floodlights, in front of eight thousand people.

During the war years of the 1940s, the Boston Red Sox kept one of their farm clubs close by at Fraser Field, as the Lynn Red Sox took up residence at the stadium.

In the 1970s Fraser Field nearly became a major league park when the proposed World Baseball League (WBL) chose the stadium as the home of its New England representative. The WBL was intended to be

ROLLER POLO

Early in the twentieth century a sport called roller polo was popular. Using basically the same set of rules as ice hockey, the game was played using roller skates on a wooden surface. The "stick" resembled a mallet. Roller polo was successful in a few New England cities. Newport, Rhode Island, was considered the hotbed, while teams were also located in Bridgeport, Connecticut; Maynard, Massachusetts, where it was played in the Music Hall; and in Lynn, Massachusetts, at the Lynn Sports Arena at 766 Western Avenue, near Magrane Square.

direct competition for the existing National and American Leagues, but neither the league nor the team ever came into existence.

In 1980 minor league ball returned as the Lynn Sailors were established in the Eastern League; they served as a farm team for the Seattle Mariners. After switching their affiliation to the Pittsburgh Pirates, the franchise later moved to Vermont. According to a present-day minor league team, the Akron Aeros of Ohio, that club is a direct descendant of the Sailors.

In the 1990s the city of Lynn was represented in the minor North Atlantic Baseball League at Fraser by the Massachusetts Mad Dogs. Coaching duties were performed by former Red Sox star George Scott. After a few years of operation and a league switch, the team folded.

In 2002 Fraser Field once again became host to minor league baseball. The North Shore Spirit, an independent team, joined the Northeast League and moved into the city of Lynn. Their chief rival is a team called the Brockton Rox, which plays in brand-new Campanelli Stadium in Brockton, Massachusetts.

BC'S ALUMNI STADIUM

PROFESSIONAL TENANTS:
Boston Patriots (American Football League); football, 1969
Boston Astros (American Soccer League); *soccer, 1970*
Boston Minutemen (North American Soccer League); *soccer, 1974*
CAPACITY: 44,500 (current); 32,000 (former)

Boston College's Alumni Stadium, also known as "the Heights," is located in Chestnut Hill. The park is the home of the highly successful Boston College Eagles football team. Winning such traditional New

Year's Day games as the Sugar Bowl and Cotton Bowl, the team has always attracted a local audience beyond students and alumni.

As a large stadium near the center of Boston, it has been the temporary home of many local sports franchises. In 1969, the Boston Patriots moved there following a six-year stint at Fenway Park. The following year the Boston Astros of the American Soccer League spent a season in Chestnut Hill, before moving on to Nickerson Field. In 1974, the area welcomed yet another soccer team to Boston College, as the Boston Minutemen of the North American League took up residence, before they too moved on to Nickerson.

WALTER BROWN ARENA
PROFESSIONAL TENANT:
Boston Lobsters (World Team Tennis); *tennis, 1974–1978*
CAPACITY: 3,806

Walter A. Brown Arena Memorial Skating Pavilion is home to the Terriers of Boston University. The hockey team has seen much success, winning several Eastern Collegiate Athletic Conference, Beanpot, and national titles. The arena has been a friendly home to the Terriers; they have won 75 percent of their home games, from the rink's opening in 1971 to the end of the twentieth century.

The venue is named for well-known local sports legend Walter Brown, who throughout his career was closely associated with Boston Arena and Boston Garden, as well as the Boston Celtics.

In addition to hockey, Brown Arena has hosted basketball games, concerts, and special events. From 1974 through 1978 it was home to the local entry into the World Team Tennis League, an experiment in the team concept for a game traditionally thought of in terms of individuals. The league, formed by such luminaries as Billie Jean King and her husband, Larry, started with franchises strung across the continent as well as from Hawaii. Games consisted of singles and doubles matches for both men and women, as well as a mixed-doubles match.

In the first year of action the chief rivals of the Boston Lobsters were the Philadelphia Freedom, Baltimore Banners, and New York Sets. The Lobsters, under the leadership of player-coach Ion Tiriac and owner Ray Ciccolo, performed well enough to finish third of five teams in their division. In the second year they were defeated by the Pittsburgh Triangles in the semifinals. After a dismal last-place finish in 1976 the

Lobsters added such stars as Martina Navratilova and Tony Roche, rebounded, and topped the standings in the team's last two years of operation.

VOLPE CENTER

PROFESSIONAL TENANTS:
Boston Comets; *teamball, 1977*
New England Gulls (Women's Professional Basketball Association); *basketball, 1980–1981*
CAPACITY: 3,617

The S. Peter Volpe Center, on the campus of Merrimack College in North Andover, is currently home to the Merrimack Warriors. Built in 1972, it houses the college's hockey rink, gymnasium, and training rooms. A three-million-dollar expansion in 2001 added luxury boxes and a VIP room.

In 1977 and 1981 the arena was the site of two experiments in professional sports, both short-lived. In 1977 an attempt was made to start a "teamball" league, loosely based on team handball. The local entry, playing at Volpe, was known as the Boston Comets.

Then in 1980 the college hosted a new franchise in the three-year-old Women's Professional Basketball Association. The New England Gulls were coached by a former Boston Celtic great, Jim Loscutoff. The Gulls did not complete their only season.

Both teams lacked sufficient funding to operate a second year.

BOWDITCH FIELD

PROFESSIONAL TENANTS:
Boston Storm (United Soccer League); *soccer, 1994–1995*
Boston Tornado (United Soccer Leagues' W-League); *soccer, 1995*
Boston Renegades (United Soccer Leagues' W-League); *soccer, 1996–present*
Boston Bulldogs (United Soccer Leagues' A-League); *soccer, 1998–2000*
CAPACITY: 5,600

Bowditch Field is home to Framingham High School's sports teams (in Framingham, Massachusetts) and has played host to many statewide athletic and musical tournaments. In addition, it has been the home of four professionally run sports organizations since the 1990s.

TWO CHAMPIONS

August 10, 2002, was a big night for Massachusetts Premier Soccer, Inc., as two of its teams won national championships, playing at the same time on opposite ends of the continent. The Boston Renegades beat the Charlotte Lady Eagles for their second consecutive title, in the finals at Vancouver, British Columbia. At the same time the firm's Division Four Men's professional team, the Cape Cod Crusaders, beat back the Boulder Rapids in Yarmouth, Massachusetts.

Beginning in 1994 a soccer team called the Boston Storm began playing at the small stadium on Union Avenue. It played in the men's division of an organization today called the United Soccer Leagues. That group operates several national leagues, including professional men's teams at the second-, third-, and fourth-division levels. A women's group, known today as the "W-League," is under the same umbrella. Until the formation of the Women's United Soccer Association in 2001, that organization was the highest level of competitive women's soccer in the country.

During the second year of the Storm's existence it formed a sister club, the Boston Tornado, placing them in the W-League.

In 1996 the men's team disbanded, but Massachusetts Premier Soccer, Inc., bought the women's club. Renamed the Boston Renegades, it began a very successful run as one of the nation's strongest clubs. In 1998 the team and Bowditch Field played host to the national championship, with the Renegades earning a berth in the semifinals. In 2001 the team went all the way, beating the Vancouver Breakers in a rain-soaked championship final.

In 1998 Massachusetts Premier Soccer moved its Worcester Wildfire east to Bowditch. Playing in the USL's A-League as the Boston Bulldogs, they were just one tier below the New England Revolution of Major League Soccer.

LOWELL'S STADIUMS

The 1990s saw a resurging interest in minor league sports, and a construction boom in fan-friendly sports venues. The city of Lowell, Massachusetts, benefited twice.

LeLacheur Park

PROFESSIONAL TENANT:

Lowell Spinners (New York Penn League); *baseball, 1998–present*

LeLacheur Park opened on June 20, 1998, at a cost of eleven million dollars. Its prime professional tenant is the Lowell Spinners team of the New York Penn Baseball League, a single-A affiliate of the Boston Red Sox; the team also manages the stadium. The Spinners, beginning their days at nearby Alumni Stadium, have proven to be an extremely popular attraction, selling out most games. In addition to having the Spinners serve as a feeder club, the Red Sox have taken advantage of the proximity of Lowell to Boston and have used the Spinners to help rehabilitate injured players.

Tsongas Arena

PROFESSIONAL TENANT:

Lowell Lock Monsters (American Hockey League); *hockey, 1998–present*

Tsongas Arena, long a dream of Lowell native and former U.S. Senator Paul Tsongas, opened on January 27, 1998, and is managed by outside arena specialists. The Mile of Mills Riverwalk, a footpath developed jointly by the city and the National Park Service, connects both the arena and LeLacheur Park with the downtown area, and was built in conjunction with the two sports venues. It also provides access to many of Lowell's historic attractions. The total cost of the rink was twenty-eight million dollars, of which the city paid four million.

On the evening of October 9, 1998, the Lowell Lock Monsters joined the American Hockey League as an affiliate of the New York Islanders. After several successful seasons, their affiliation was switched to the Carolina Hurricanes.

The River Hawks of the University of Lowell also play their games at Tsongas, which can accommodate sixty-five hundred hockey fans and up to seven thousand for concerts and other events.

Cawley Stadium

PROFESSIONAL TENANT:

Boston Cannons (National Lacrosse League); *lacrosse, 2001–present*

CAPACITY: 5,137

Cawley Stadium on Douglas Road in Lowell is home to the Lowell High School football team as well as the Keith Academy club. In 1935, the Cawley family donated nearly fourteen acres to the city and to the Lowell High School Alumni Association, for the express purpose of placing an athletic facility there. Built in 1937 as a WPA project, it was initially named "Alumni Stadium"; during the Second World War it became known as "Lowell Memorial Stadium," until in 1966 the city recognized the original benefactors. In a dedication ceremony, the park was named in honor of Edward J. Cawley, who was a high-school grid-iron star and later played baseball for the Philadelphia Athletics.

A cement grandstand measuring 50 feet by 360 feet supports metal seating for 4,137 people, while a smaller visitors' stand holds an additional 1,000 seats.

In 2001, the Boston Cannons joined the National Lacrosse League and began playing at the park against such opposition as the Long Island Lizards, Rochester Rattlers, and Bridgeport Barrage. The Cannons fin-

---

WOMEN'S FOOTBALL

At the start of the twenty-first century the Boston area was supporting two women's football teams. The first, known as the New England Storm, play in the Women's Professional Football League (WPFL). Owned by Melissa Korpacz, the team began life in Providence, Rhode Island. In its first year of operation the Storm nearly made it to the top, losing Championship Game I to the Houston Energy by a score of 39–7. In 2002 the team moved closer to the Boston area, to Hormel Stadium in Medford. Its new field, within sight of Interstate Route 93, and just five miles north of Boston, was built by the Metropolitan District Commission, and opened in May 1966. Price tag to the state was $552,073. It is named for Henry D. Hormel, a former member of the MDC Park Commission. He had also worked for the city of Medford as an athlete, coach, and teacher.

The National Women's Football League, also formed in 2000, was the brainchild of sports entrepreneur Catherine Masters. The new league included the local team, Mass Mutiny. Consisting of more than twenty players and the head coach from the Storm, the new team had a successful start. Playing at Lawrence Stadium near the junction of Interstate 495 and Route 114 in Lawrence, twenty miles north of Boston, the Mutiny made it to the first-ever set of semifinals, losing only to the eventual champion Philadelphia Liberty Belles.

In the second year of operation, Mass Mutiny moved down I-495 a few miles, to Cushing Field at the University of Massachusetts in Lowell.

ished second their first season, securing a play-off spot, but they lost in the championship semifinals.

OLYMPICS IN BOSTON?

Throughout Boston's history many professional sports venues have been planned but never built. No set of plans has been as intriguing or as intricate as those created by the Boston Olympic Organizing Committee. The group was established to explore the possibility of staging the quadrennial event in the Hub from July 15 through August 3 in 2008.

Although the plans were never executed, and the Twenty-Ninth Summer Games were eventually awarded to Beijing, the blueprint for hosting them locally makes for interesting reading.

Satellite Venues

The committee felt that the area's abundance of college and professional facilities made it feasible to host the Olympics without needing to build many new parks and arenas. Of the twenty-six principal venues necessary, it was felt that twenty-two existing structures could be used with little or no modification.

In the preliminary report, the committee created a tentative list of sites, including Tufts University (archery), the Hynes Convention Center (badminton), Fenway Park (baseball), the Worcester Centrum and the Fleet-Center (basketball), either the Concord River or the Charles River (canoeing), Herter Park on the Charles River (modern pentathlon), the Wang Center (weightlifting), and Camp Curtis Guild in Reading (shooting).

Other possible sites included Matthews Arena, Longwood Cricket Club, Reggie Lewis Center, Conte Forum, and Boston Common.

Olympic Stadium

Four proposals were reviewed for the building of an Olympic Stadium, intended to house opening and closing ceremonies as well as track-and-field events.

The first was called the "berm stadium." It consisted of berm earthworks, which would accommodate spectator seating for approximately forty-three thousand fans and surround the track. Above the amphitheater was to be a temporary steel-framed tier, holding an additional twenty-three thousand seats. After the games, the steel tier would be removed, leaving only the lower portion. The second possibility was a "demountable" temporary stadium, holding seventy thousand spectators, to be completely removed following the closing ceremonies. The third idea called for a more permanent structure, on a smaller lot of land, but accommodating the same-sized crowd by creating several levels. The three proposals targeted possible sites in Allston, Cambridge, and along the Fort Point Channel.

The fourth proposal was actually a modification of a plan already in existence when the Olympic Organizing Committee was investigating possibilities: it called for a slight modification of the Boston Redevelopment Authority's planned South Bay Megaplex. The Megaplex never happened. Likewise, after encountering many obstacles, the Boston committee put its dream of hosting the Olympics on hold indefinitely.

OLYMPIC LOGO

The Boston Olympic logo consisted of a torch overlaid on a silhouette of the Old North Church steeple. The steeple was framed by a star, which in turn was boxed, with the words "Boston, USA," appearing several times behind the stars. According to the organizing committee, it represented "the historical significance of Boston as a founding city of our nation and as a cradle of freedom and human rights. The Old North Church represents Paul Revere's and William Dawes' famous rides ..."

BOSTON'S FIRSTS AND FOREMOSTS

In 1897 the Boston Athletic Association held the first Boston Marathon, today the oldest annual marathon in the world.

The Davis Cup Tournament, emblematic of men's tennis team championship, began in Boston in 1900. Harvard student Dwight Filley Davis challenged an English team to a match and commissioned Shreve, Crump, and Lowe to fashion a trophy for the winner. Today 129 nations compete annually for the Davis Cup. The tournament site has moved around the world, but the first edition of the tournament was hosted in Massachusetts by the Longwood Cricket Club.

The first modern World Series, pitting Boston against Pittsburgh, was played at the Huntington Avenue Grounds in 1903. The World Series has also been played at two other sites in Boston: Fenway Park (1912, 1914, 1918, 1946, 1967, 1975, and 1986) and Braves Field (1915, 1916, and 1948).

Harvard Stadium, built in 1903, is the oldest collegiate sports venue in the country.

Two baseball games are noted in the record books as the first perfect game; both claims are made with sound reasoning and both occurred in Massachusetts. In 1880 Lee Richmond faced and retired twenty-seven men in Worcester. Cy Young performed the same feat at Boston's Huntington Avenue Grounds in 1904. Baseball statistics compiled after 1900 have always been considered "modern" records, making Young's the first modern perfect game.

Matthews Arena, originally known as "Boston Arena," opened in 1910 and is the oldest indoor ice arena in the world.

Fenway Park, built in 1912, is the oldest baseball field in the major leagues.

The Northeastern University campus in Boston contains the sites of the South End Grounds, the Huntington Avenue Grounds, and Boston Arena (today known as "Matthews Arena"). In all, these venues were the birthplaces of nine major league teams, five of which still exist today.

Boston University's Nickerson Field is part of the former Braves Field, home to the Boston Braves from 1915 to 1952. Three World Series were played at the site.

Playing at Boston Arena, the Boston Bruins were the first American team to join the National Hockey League (1924–25 season).

In 1954 Boston Garden became the first NHL arena to use a Zamboni machine to resurface the ice. That machine is now in the Hockey Hall of Fame in Toronto.

Calling Boston Garden home, the Boston Celtics won more NBA championship banners than any other team. The record sixteen victories include eight consecutive wins, from 1959 through 1966.

Both Major League Soccer (men) and the Women's United Soccer Association chose Foxboro Stadium to host their respective inaugural championship games. The MLS Cup final took place in 1996 and the WUSA Founder's Cup match in 2001.

Boston's baseball parks have been home to four National Football League teams. The Bulldogs and Braves played at Braves Field; the Braves, renamed the Redskins, played at Fenway Park, as did the Yanks and Patriots.

During the 2001 NFL season the New England Patriots completed a "worst to first" run. After finishing the previous year in last place with a record of five wins and eleven losses, the team turned it around, finishing with eleven wins and five losses. Behind second-string quarterback Tom Brady the Patriots went all the way, winning the Super Bowl crown in January 2002.

BIBLIOGRAPHY

Unless otherwise indicated, all newspapers
are from Massachusetts towns.

American Heritage Dictionary of the English Language. Boston:
    Houghton Mifflin Co., 1976.
Anderson, Will R. *Tessie.* New York: M. Whitmark & Sons, 1902.
Andover Townsman, 1922–1926.
Boston Chronicle, 1932–1950.
Boston Globe, 1872–1998.
Boston Guardian, 1940 (various issues).
Boston Journal, 1870–1899.
Boston Herald, 1870–1960.
Boston Olympic Organizing Committee. *Bringing the Games to Boston.*
    Pamphlet, Boston, undated.
Boston Post, 1870–1910, 1940.
Boston Transcript. 24 April 1923, 16 September 1924.
Boston Traveler, 28 April 1923.
Boston University Athletic Department archives, Boston, Mass.
BU Bridge (Boston University), 12 September 1997.
Chicago Tribune, Chicago, Ill., 1880 (various issues).
Daily Beacon (University of Tennessee at Knoxville), 28 September
    1995.
Fall River Globe, 1921–1931.
Foulds, Samuel T. N., and Paul Harris. *America's Soccer Heritage.*
    Manhattan Beach, Calif.: Soccer For Americans, 1979.
Grinold, Jack (Sports Information Director, Northeastern University,
    Boston, Mass.). Interview, August 2002, Boston.
Holway, John. *The Complete Book of Baseball's Negro Leagues: The Other
    Half of Baseball History.* Fern Park, Fla.: Hastings House, 2001.
Honolulu Star Bulletin, Honolulu, Hawaii, 17 June–8 July 1997.
Johnson, Richard, and Glenn Stout. *The Red Sox Century.* Boston:
    Houghton Mifflin, 2000.
Jose, Colin. *American Soccer League 1921–1931.* Lanham, Miss.:
    Scarecrow Press, 1998.

Kelly, J. W. *Slide, Kelly, Slide!* New York: Frank Harding, 1889.

Kountze, Mabry. *Fifty Sports Years Down Memory Lane*. Medford, Mass.: Mystic Valley Press, 1979.

Lawrence Eagle Tribune, 1925.

Lynn Daily Evening Item, 1923–1940.

Malden Evening News, 18 April–20 April 1925.

McCauley, Peter. *Greetings from Revere Beach*. Revere, Mass.: Peter McCauley, 1978.

McCauley, Peter. *Memories of Revere Beach*. Revere, Mass.: Peter McCauley, 1989.

McCauley, Peter. *Pictorial History of Revere Beach*. Revere, Mass.: Peter McCauley, 1980.

McGreevey, Michael. McGreevey Scrapbook. Boston Public Library archives. Boston, undated.

Merrimack College Athletic Department archives, North Andover, Mass.

Metropolitan District Commission Office of Policy archives, Boston, Mass.

National League Nostalgia Series. Worcester vs. Troy. Program, Wellesley, Mass.: Wellesley Press, 22 June 1992.

New York Times, New York, N.Y., 1890 (various issues).

O'Neil, Buck. *I Was Right On Time*. New York: Simon & Schuster, 1996.

Philadelphia Inquirer, Philadelphia, Pa., 1883; 1903–1904.

Providence Journal, Providence, R.I., 1880; 8 May 2002.

Roddy, Edward G. *Mills, Mansions, and Mergers—The Life of William M. Wood*. North Andover, Mass.: Merrimack Valley Textile Museum, 1982.

Russo, Frank. "Beer Drinkers and Hellraisers." http://www.thedeadball era.com (accessed 12 May 2004).

Ryczek, William J. *Blackguards and Redstockings*. Wallingford, Conn.: Colebrook Press, 1992.

Sanborn Insurance Company. Various maps. 1890–1938.

Soos, Troy. *Before the Curse*. Hyannis, Mass.: Parnassus Imprints, 1997.

Sporting News. 1904 (various issues).

Treat, Roger. *The Encyclopedia of Football*, 12th ed. New York: A. S. Barnes & Co., 1974.

Turkin, Hy, and S. C. Thompson. *The Official Encyclopedia of Baseball*, 9th ed. New York: Doubleday & Co., 1977.

Woodworth, Anne H. *Soccer Zones*. Birmingham, Mich.: Soccer Prose, Inc., 1994.

Worcester Aegis & Telegram, 1879–1883.
Worcester Daily Spy, 1870–1883.
Worcester Whistleblower, 10 May 1990–27 September 1990.

ACKNOWLEDGMENTS

Any book that covers a wide time span, and deals, in some cases, with obscure pieces of history, requires the help of many people to produce. *Boston's Ballparks and Arenas* is no exception. The author would like to thank and acknowledge the following people and organizations that helped uncover much of Boston's sports past:

My wife, Anna Carroll Foulds, who was there at every step, from digging through old newspapers and archives to helping catch typos and creating an index; my daughter, Amanda Foulds, who, with Anna, spent hours reviewing and critiquing the first draft; John Landrigan of UPNE and my friend Liz Nelson, who shaped my writing into the book it became; Mike Hartnett for his background information on the workings of the Boston Garden; Bijan Bayne, Mel King, Tracy McDaniel, Kevin Paul Dupont, Edward Downes, the Sanborn Map Company, and Gordon Edes for their help in finding Lincoln Park and those who played there; Thomas R. BelleGarde, Lowell Parks and Recreation, and Peter Aucella, National Park Service, for their information on Lowell's stadiums; Sarah Mercer of Harvard's Sports Information office; Jack Grinold of Northeastern University's Sports Information office for sharing his extensive historical knowledge of Boston Arena; the staff at the Boston Public Library microfilm department; the Massachusetts Historical Society and William Fowler, its director; Richard Foulds for digging through the Philadelphia Public Library for information on Rube Waddell and the Philadelphia Athletics; Dianne M. Foulds, who expertly took photographs for me wherever and whenever I needed them; Dianne Foulds, Lillian Foulds, and Jackie and Nick Spada for unrestricted use of their photo collections; Brian Goslow for information on Worcester's brief stay in the major leagues; Julie Mofford and the Andover Historical Society for background on Shawsheen Village; Arthur Foulds for his knowledge of Revere Beach, GE Field, and Lynn roller polo; Paul Boothroyd for information on Maynard's roller polo team; Colin Jose of the National Soccer Hall of Fame; the *Boston Globe*; the *Boston Herald*; the *Daily Item* (Lynn, Mass.); Dan Griffin and the *Lawrence Eagle Tribune*; the *Andover Townsman*; Bill Ballou of the *Worcester Telegram*; Domenic D'Ambrosio and Sean Fisher of the Metropolitan District Commission, for Medford stadium history; Dan Wilson and Save Fenway Park!; Massachusetts Premier Soccer; the

ACKNOWLEDGMENTS

Lynn Historical Society; Peter McCauley; Carin O'Connor of the Boston Public Library, Dudley Square branch; Ben Steinberg of the Brookline Public Library; Joanne Callahan, Boston Parks and Recreation; Ellen Jacobs of the Somerville Public Library; the Fall River Public Library; Wallace Kountze; the Lynn Public Library; the Boston Cannons Lacrosse Club; the New England Storm Football Club; the Mass Mutiny Football Club; Dick Curtis for technical assistance; Richard Johnson and the New England Sports Museum; William Burdick and the National Baseball Hall of Fame and Museum; Robyn Christensen and the Worcester Historical Museum; Nancy Richard of the Bostonian Society; Aaron Schmidt, who has done so much for the preservation of Boston's sports temple history at the Boston Public Library; the Sam Foulds Collection; and, from the past, Michael "Nuf Ced" McGreevey, whose amazing collection of baseball photographs lives on long after the stadiums he chronicled.

INDEX

211